A Mother's
DAILY
PRAYER
BOOK

Elaine Creasman
June Eaton
Margaret Anne Huffman
Marie D. Jones

Publications International, Ltd.

Elaine Creasman is a writer for dozens of religious magazines and publications and has contributed to such books as *Treasury of God's Virtues* and *How to Let God Help You Through Hard Times*. She was given the 1991 Writer of the Year Award by the Florida Christian Writers Conference.

June Eaton is a teacher and freelance writer whose published work includes Sunday school curriculum as well as stories and articles in more than 50 Christian publications. She has also contributed to many books, including *The Bible: A to Z, This Too Shall Pass*, and *Heartwarmers: Moms Are the Best*.

Margaret Anne Huffman is an award-winning journalist and former lifestyle editor of the *Shelby News*. She has written and contributed to many books, including *Simple Wisdom, A Moment with God for Mothers*, and *Everyday Prayers for Grandmothers*.

Marie D. Jones is widely published in both books and magazines and has contributed to such titles as *The Silver Book of Hope* and *Bless This Marriage*.

PHOTO CREDIT:
Cover: **Shutterstock.com**

Louis Weber, CEO
Publications International, Ltd.
8140 Lehigh Avenue
Morton Grove, Illinois 60053

Permission is never granted for commercial purposes.

ISBN: 978-1-4508-9936-9

Manufactured in China.

8 7 6 5 4 3 2 1

Talking With God

Imagine if you had a direct channel to the creator of the universe. Imagine if you could just speak—or think—and he would hear you. More than that, he would listen. What would you say? Your answer, of course—whatever it is—would be prayer.

Aside from listening to God's message to us, there may be no greater opportunity available to human beings than talking directly to God through prayer. It allows us to express our faith, and the more we talk, the more we realize that God works in us through those conversations far beyond the requests we bring. He uses our own prayers to draw us closer to him, to help us see him more clearly. What's more, by accepting our pleases and thank-yous and hallelujahs—and actively responding to them—God uses prayer as a way to show the great love he has for his children.

This book of daily prayers has been specifically designed as a tool for mothers who talk to God. It includes prayers—both formal and informal, classic and modern—on a wide variety of subjects that affect moms, from balancing the roles of mother and wife to teaching children about God, and from the power of prayer to dealing with kids' temper tantrums! Some days feature prayers of thanksgiving; other days offer requests for God's guidance; and still others will lead you in prayers of praise to God for his grace, mercy, or creative genius. In addition to the daily prayer, most days will also include a brief passage from scripture and an inspirational quote.

None of the prayers included in *A Mother's Daily Prayer Book* contain language or structure that make them more acceptable or effective than any sincere communication from one of God's children. They are simply offered as a starting place. Each can be prayed word for word or used as a blueprint for the reader's own, more specific prayer. Feel free to make these prayers your own as you personally dialogue with God.

Additionally, at the end of each month you will find a blank page titled "My Prayer Life." These spaces have been set aside for you to write specific requests, items of praise and thanks, or notes about what God is teaching you through prayer and his Word.

Our hope is that *A Mother's Daily Prayer Book* will help you take advantage of the awesome privilege of talking with God every day. Enjoy.

January 1

But I trust in you, O Lord; I say, "You are my God."
My times are in your hand.

Psalm 31:14–15

Lord, you have created the earth and set it spinning in its orbit. You have established the seasons by which we measure the years. As this new year beckons, my times and those of my children are truly in your hands. Help me in my resolve to be a better, more understanding parent. Guide me in my mothering, and though I sometimes stumble, assure me that you will always be here to keep me on course.

Each new year is like a young child, full of possibilities and promises. In the coming months, help me to make the most of each opportunity to encourage my children, to deal more patiently with them, and to teach them of your unfailing love. You are the God for all times, for all eternity.

Children carry a promise with them,
a hidden treasure that has to be led
into the open through education
in a hospitable home.

—Henri J. M. Nouwen, *Reaching Out*

January 2

Take heart . . . your sins are forgiven.

Matthew 9:2

Father, the beginning of a new year speaks of a fresh start and new opportunities. It is a good time to teach our children about forgiveness and trying again when we have failed.

We are thankful that you are a God of second chances. Just as you love us unconditionally, there is nothing our children could do to make us stop loving them. Help us teach them the hopeful message that there is no need for despair; that forgiveness and a new start are always possible.

Forgiveness is the first step
on the road to a fresh start.

January 3

My child . . . do not forsake your mother's teaching. Bind them upon your heart always; tie them around your neck. When you walk, they will lead you; when you lie down, they will watch over you; and when you awake, they will talk with you.

Proverbs 6:20–22

have such good intentions, Lord of promise, but sometimes I slip in carrying them out. Guide my actions so that they match my words as I make footprints for my children to follow. Make me worthy of being a pathfinder. Amen.

The religion of a child depends upon what its mother and father are, and not what they say.

—Henri Frederic Amiel

January 4

Lord, as I look into my small children's faces, I wonder what their futures will be. Though I often complain of the routines of our daily life, I know these are the uncomplicated days. As the children grow and go out into the world, how will I protect them from the forces that would harm them? How can I guard them against the hurt feelings, disappointments, and negative influences of people who do not love them as I do?

Heavenly Father, I cling to your promise that you have a plan for their lives and will give each of them a future filled with hope. I thank you that you hear me when I come to you in prayer. I rely on your word that you will protect these precious little ones who embody my hopes for the future.

Hope is faith holding out its hand in the dark.

—George Iles

January 5

Speak, Lord, for your servant is listening.

1 Samuel 3:9

Lord, speak to me, that I may speak
    In living echoes of thy tone;
As thou hast sought, so let me seek
Thine erring children lost and lone.

O teach me, Lord, that I may teach
The precious things thou dost impart;
And wing my words, that they may reach
The hidden depths of many a heart.

O fill me with thy fullness, Lord,
Until my very heart o'erflow
In kindling thought and glowing
    word,
Thy love to tell, thy praise to show.

—Frances R. Havergal

*To have God's words inscribed on your heart
is to be armed for all the world's battles.*

January 6

I can do all things through him who strengthens me.

Philippians 4:13

Lord, I am overwhelmed with the whirl of activity around me. Getting the children up and dressed, making breakfast, taking them to school, doing dishes, cleaning house, running errands, fielding phone calls, meeting appointments, retrieving the kids, supervising homework, delivering them to music lessons and sports practices, dealing with calamities . . . how do I fit it all in? I am buckling under the weight of each day, only to find that I must get up and start all over again the next.

Father, you are a God of peace and tranquility. I long to find a time to sit down and talk to you. Show me a quiet place in the midst of the frenzy, where I may commune with you, be refreshed, and know that through your strength, I can accomplish all that you have set out for me to do today.

As a mother, I must faithfully, patiently, lovingly and happily do my part—then quietly wait for God to do His.

—Ruth Bell Graham, *Prodigals and Those Who Love Them*

January 7

He said to them, "Is a lamp brought in to be put under the bushel basket, or under the bed, and not on the lampstand?"

Mark 4:21

Thank you, God of inspiration, for the times when you guide me to take my place as an example and a model for my children. For you call us to be loving, tender, and kind. Remind me that this call is more than just creating a family, for the family is Christianity in miniature.

There are two ways of spreading light: to be the candle or the mirror that reflects it.

—Edith Wharton

January 8

All your children shall be taught by the Lord,
and great shall be the prosperity of your children.

Isaiah 54:13

Protect and guide my beloved children.... Let them always feel Your faithful presence wherever they go and in all their undertakings. When they are confused, I pray they will wait for Your clarity. When they are afraid, I pray they will seek Your soothing calm. When they are alone, I pray they will feel Your loving presence. When they are sick, I pray You will lay Your healing hand upon them. When they are tired and overwrought, please lead them to Your still waters of calm and restore their spirits. When they face disappointments and dashed hopes and friends and foe alike abandon them, let them find refuge in Your never-changing faithfulness and love.

—Marian Wright Edelman, *Guide My Feet*

Father, a new baby puts such demands on me that I am reeling under the pressure. Round-the-clock feedings, endless diaper changes, and loss of sleep have made me feel depressed.

I love my baby, Lord, and cherish being a mother, but I am losing myself. I spend every waking moment focusing on this child, listening for sounds of hunger, discomfort, or displeasure.

Please forgive my self-pity and resentment, Lord. I don't mean to complain, but the transition has been a shock. Restore my sense of balance and my sense of humor. Help me to find rest so I can function as a normal person once again.

Guide me through this confusing stage of motherhood so I can function as the cheerful, loving parent I was meant to be.

Self-pity is like a thief in the night, robbing us of our joy.

January 10

For I have set you an example,
that you also should do as I have done to you.

John 13:15

Lord, make me a model of your love, a fitting example from which my children can learn how to live. Help me to keep my thoughts and words pure, always pleasing in your sight.

In a world where deception is commonplace, fill me with truth and honesty so I may avoid making empty promises and sending conflicting signals. May my actions always model the message of my words.

Grant me your patience and understanding so that I may listen with my heart to my children's true feelings.

Teach me to control my temper so I may provide for my children peace of mind rather than "a piece of my mind."

Season me with gentleness, kindness, and forgiveness so my family can experience through me the joy and richness of life with you.

Example is not the main thing in influencing others.
It is the only thing.

—Albert Schweitzer

January 11

Creator, help me to remember who I am. Before I became a friend, there was me. Before I became a wife, there was me. Before I became a mother, there was me. Guide me back to that person that I gave away so long ago. Give me back to "me," and restore my wholeness, so that I can then become a better friend, a better wife, and a better mother. Direct me back onto the path you set out for me so long ago, before I got sidetracked by the roles and duties of life. Help me, Lord, help me find my way back home again.

January 12

Then the Lord God said, "It is not good that the man should be alone; I will make him a helper as his partner."

Genesis 2:18

Our Spiritual Father, grant to this couple true love to unite them spiritually, patience to assimilate their differences, forgiveness to cover their failures, guidance to lead them in the proper ways, courage to face perplexity, and inner peace to comfort and uphold them even in disillusionment and distress throughout their lives. In Jesus' Name. Amen.

—James L. Christensen,
New Ways to Worship

Two persons must believe in each other, and feel that it can be done and must be done; that way they are enormously strong. They must keep each other's courage up.

—Vincent van Gogh

January 13

I give thanks to you, O Lord my God, with my whole heart, and I will glorify your name forever.

Psalm 86:12

Lord, you are the God who has set the foundations of the earth, who blessed Abraham with offspring "as numerous as the stars in heaven." You have blessed me, too, by giving me the treasure of my heart: my family. I pour out my thanks for these gifts, which are far above any riches the world can give. How can I praise you enough?

Heavenly Father, I never fail to come to you for help and comfort in the dark times of my life, yet I don't always remember you when my cup is overflowing. Forgive me if I seem ungrateful and take your generosity for granted. How can I forget all that you give me each day?

You bring beauty, peace, and love to my existence. My heart overflows with thanksgiving.

Thou that has given so much to me,
give one thing more: a grateful heart.

—George Herbert

January 14

By wisdom a house is built, and by understanding it is established;
by knowledge the rooms are filled with all precious and pleasant riches.

Proverbs 24:3–4

Heavenly Father, your word tells us that wisdom, understanding, and knowledge are the tools we need to build our home and family. We desire for our children the pleasant riches that you promise, but we aren't always sure which ways are right.

How do we develop the knowledge and understanding? How do we acquire the necessary wisdom all at once? It takes time, Lord, and reliance on you.

Yours is the wisdom we need to banish selfishness and make life less difficult for each other. Your understanding can help us look out for one another and love each other unconditionally. Your knowledge will show us how to handle our problems and live comfortably in the world.

Teach us your truths, O Lord. Show us what we need to know to establish our home and to fill it with happiness and contentment.

A happy home and family are the source
of the greatest human happiness.

January 15

For the commandment is a lamp and the teaching a light,
and the reproofs of discipline are the way of life.

Proverbs 6:23

I know the children need guidance and correction, Lord. I want to be appropriate in both, and so, I look to you for an even-handed, upbuilding approach. In this way, they are assured love and, at the same time, boundaries, expectations, responsibilities, and consequences.

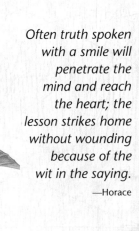

Often truth spoken
with a smile will
penetrate the
mind and reach
the heart; the
lesson strikes home
without wounding
because of the
wit in the saying.

—Horace

January 16

God,

Allow me to be the kind of mother that my child can be proud of.

Allow me to be the kind of friend that my child will turn to.

Allow me to be the kind of mentor that my child will seek advice from.

Allow me to be the kind of guardian that will protect my child from harm.

But, also, God, allow me to be the kind of person who knows that my child, like me, has been given the gift of freedom, the freedom to risk, to make mistakes, and even to fail.

Allow me to be the kind of parent that my child would one day like to be.

Amen.

January 17

*Do not worry about anything, but in everything
by prayer and supplication with thanksgiving
let your requests be made known to God.*

Philippians 4:6

I confess, Lord, that in my haste to come to
you in prayer and to present my daily
laundry list of requests, I forget the other side of
prayer. I forget to listen for your answer. I know that if
I am patient enough, your gentle message will come to
me when I wait for it.

Forgive me my impatience, Father, when I ask for
your help with my children, then fail to listen to your
response. Thank you for teaching me that if I seek, I
will find. Help me to seek and listen for your answers,
written across the pages of my heart.

*When we pray,
we tell God what he already knows.
When we listen,
God tells us what we should know.*

January 18

Keep these words . . . in your heart. Recite them to your children and talk about them when you are at home and when you are away, when you lie down and when you rise.

Deuteronomy 6:6–7

Loving God, I have dedicated my children to you and have promised to teach them your laws. Sometimes I feel ineloquent, inadequate, unfit for the task. But you are with me, Lord; you can supply what I lack.

I long to show my loved ones how to walk daily in your light, to bask in your warmth, and to love you with all of their hearts.

Please grant me the understanding I need to show each child how to worship and obey you, so they may experience the joy of your presence in their lives.

Your love fills me with song, O Lord. Help me teach the words to my children.

God never gives us the light which our children need;
he keeps it for them.

—Henry Ward Beecher, *Life Thoughts*

January 19

Lord, with all my
  heart I thank You
For a trusting teenager
Who is sufficiently secure
  and mature
To seek parental guidance.
Last night she approached
  me directly:
"Mom, I've got a real
  problem
And I need to share it
  with you."
For over an hour we
  talked
(As we've often done
  before)
Personally
Intimately
With beautiful freedom
With healthy objectivity.
All the while I prayed for
  direction.
I knew You had given it,
  Lord

When suddenly she
  grabbed my hand
Sighed deeply
And said with obvious
  relief:
"Thanks, Mom. You've
  helped.
I sort of knew you would."
Then this morning
After she'd dashed out
  the door
I found her hurriedly
  scribbled note:
"Mom: You're like a
  personal rainbow
After a storm.
Thanks—and a whole
  bunch of love."
Dear Lord
What more could a
  mother ask?

—Ruth Harms Calkin, *Keep Me Faithful*

January 20

For "In him we live and move and have our being....
For we too are his offspring."

—Acts 17:28

We thank you, Lord, who gave us sight and sense
    to smell the flowers,
to hear the wind,
to feel the waters in our hand,
to sleep with the night and wake with the sun,
to stand upon this star,
to sing your praise,
to hear your voice.

Blessed and praised
be the Lord, from
whom comes all the
good that we speak
and think and do.

—Teresa of Avila,
The Way of Perfection

January 21

God is our refuge and strength, an ever-present help in trouble.

Psalm 46:1 NIV

Job reminds us that as sure as the sparks fly upward, human beings are born to trouble. Our time of trouble is here, Lord.

We thank you for temporary relief—for giving us respite so we can gather strength for the next battle we must face.

But our sorrow is great, Father, and we can see no way out of this situation. Our hearts are heavy as we look into the future and see nothing but darkness. We are afraid for ourselves and our children.

But you take our burdens as your own. You are our refuge and strength. We will cling to you in time of trouble, knowing you can lead us step-by-step out of the darkness and into the light.

We hold to your promise to be with us wherever we go, and we will not be afraid.

God does not offer us a way out of the testings of life.
He offers us a way through.

—W. T. Purkiser

January 22

*Discipline your children, and they will give you rest;
they will give delight to your heart.*

Proverbs 29:17

Lord, it is so easy to love my children but so hard to discipline them. I want to be a good mother, but I am afraid I will stifle my youngsters' spirits with my constant correction and will cause them to turn away from me.

Please help me to find a balance between indulgence and toughness. Help me to understand that though it is painful to correct and to be corrected, discipline teaches us the right way to do things so we can live an orderly life.

I need only to look to you to find an example of a good parent, Lord. You gently correct those you love when they make mistakes. With your help, I can do the same.

Don't become overly discouraged if you have problems with your children. God understands. He has problems with His kids too.

—Gigi Graham Tchividjian, *Weather of the Heart*

January 23

Blessed are the meek, for they will inherit the earth....
Blessed are the merciful, for they will receive mercy.
Blessed are the pure in heart, for they will see God.

Matthew 5:5, 7–8

Teach me, teach me, dearest Jesus
    In thine own sweet loving way,
All the lessons of perfection
I must practice day by day.

Teach me meekness, dearest Jesus,
Of Thine own the counterpart,
Not in words and actions only,
But the meekness of the heart.

Teach humility, sweet Jesus
To this poor, proud heart of mine,
Which yet wishes, O my Jesus,
To be modelled after Thine.

—Reverend F. X. Lasance

To be the best mothers we can be requires only a willingness
to let God work through us. We may not be perfect, but as
long as we are open, humble, and willing, blessings will occur.

January 24

My dear brothers and sisters: You must all be quick to listen, slow to speak, and slow to get angry. Human anger does not produce the righteousness God desires.

James 1:19–20 NLT

Lord, I'm convinced that shopping and children don't mix. A quick trip to the grocery store can be full of so many traps. My normally agreeable children often go berserk. I can never predict which aisle will inspire outcries of "Gimme...I want..." or provoke the children's mischief against each other amid onlookers' disapproving sneers.

Why do my children choose the supermarket to display their worst manners? What am I doing wrong, Lord? Please keep me calm in the center of the chaos, and help me find you beside me at the checkout counter.

A calm spirit pours water on the hottest fire.

January 25

Therefore I tell you, do not worry about your life, what you will eat or what you will drink, or about your body, what you will wear. Is not life more than food, and the body more than clothing?

Matthew 6:25

Loving God, I confess that I worry too much. I worry about the welfare of my children. I worry about my husband's job. I worry about our budget, which buckles under the weight of our growing family. I even worry about worrying!

Forgive my doubts and my lack of faith and trust in you, O Lord. Teach me to express my family's needs to you daily in prayer and to trust in your ability to supply them.

In my heart I know you will never let us down. With you in charge of their lives, my children will want for nothing, for you take care of all your creations—even the tiniest bird and flower.

When you worry, you are borrowing problems that may never happen.

January 26

He will yet fill your mouth with laughter, and your lips with shouts of joy.

Job 8:21

here is a choice, O God, when I spot the crayon markings on the wall, the spilled food, the wet towel on the bed. I have equal breath to scream or laugh. I feel the insistent tickle of my funny bone, and I know which choice you will. Help me laugh my way into a better mood.

Angry people usually take life too seriously, so relax. Loosen up. Look at the big picture. Let go of your anger. In light of eternity, it's not worth spending your short time on earth being angry.

—Kent Crockett,
The 911 Handbook

January 27

I am the bread of life: he that cometh to me shall never hunger; and he that believeth on me shall never thirst.

John 6:35 KJV

God of providence, as I work to satisfy the hunger and thirst of my husband and children, I can feel your presence here in my kitchen, directing me and loving me. I remember with a thankful heart that you feed my family, too. I may appease their physical hunger, but you satisfy their hungry hearts with heavenly food—"the Bread of Life"—your son, Jesus Christ.

O Lord, who each day gives us our daily bread, bless my kitchen today as I use it to prepare nourishment for my family. My heart overflows as I joyfully cook and serve the meals in an act of love and worship.

Then do not grasp at the stars,
but do life's plain, common work as it comes,
certain that daily duties and daily bread
are the sweetest things in life.

—Robert Louis Stevenson

January 28

Do not set foot on the path of the wicked or walk in the way of evildoers. Avoid it, do not travel on it; turn from it and go on your way.

Proverbs 4:14–15 NIV

Lord of all that is good, I am concerned about the bad influences my children are exposed to in the media. Entertainment seems to have reached a new low, and the innocent are most vulnerable.

Good taste, integrity, and morality are thrown to the wind as TV stations and websites vie for customers with the basest of materials. It hurts to see innocence lost so soon.

Though we try to control what our youngsters see and hear in our home, we cannot always control what they are exposed to away from home.

Guard their young eyes and ears from the evils around them, Father. Help me to teach them to turn away from the unwholesome, corrupting images and to focus on your truths.

Evil enters like a needle and spreads like an oak tree.

—Ethiopian Proverb

January 29

[God] hears us every time we ask him.

1 John 5:15 NCV

Prayer, O God, is as steadying as a hand on the rudder of a free-floating boat and as reliable as sunrise after night. It keeps me going, connected as I am to you, the source of wind beneath my daily wings.

Everyone prays in their own language,
and there is no language
that God does not understand.

—Duke Ellington

Father, I know that I am not perfect, but please let my children think I come pretty close.

Let my husband know that I am the same spontaneous woman he married, even if many days seem so controlled.

Let my friends know that I am still the wild and fun-loving woman they liked to spend time with, even if we haven't gone out together in a while.

Give me the wings of infinite spirit, even if my physical body can't leave the ground, and give me the heart of a saint, especially when the temptation to sin in anger and impatience grows strong. Amen.

Instead of feeling overwrought with demands
to the point of being overwhelmed,
feel the overflowing joy that comes from daily life
in the midst of a hustling, bustling family.
The two halves make one marvelous whole
of God's balance.

For the promise you unfold
    with the opening of each day,
I thank you, Lord.
For blessings shared along the way,
I thank you, Lord.
For the comfort of our home
filled with love to keep us warm,
I thank you, Lord.
For shelter from the winter storm,
I thank you, Lord.
For the gifts of peace and grace
you grant the family snug within,
I thank you, Lord.
For shielding us from harm and sin,
I thank you, Lord.
For the beauty of the snow
sparkling in the winter sun,
I thank you, Lord.
For the peace when the day is done,
I thank you, Lord.

Each day comes bearing its own gifts.
Untie the ribbons.

—Ruth Ann Schabacker

My Prayer Life

February 1

Lord, I know we show our love for you by loving others—family, friends, and neighbors. Sometimes it is not easy, Loving God. When I am tired and the kids seem to be aliens from another planet, when I am frustrated and feel unloved myself, when I just don't seem to care, or when I am cold and harsh, warm me and help me to see others through your eyes—worth the effort to love.

Use my name often. Think of the unending call of "Mother" made by children.... Use it not only when you need help but to express love. Uttered aloud, or in the silence of your hearts, it will alter an atmosphere from one of discord to one of love. It will raise the standard of talk and thought. "Jesus."

—God Calling

February 2

Let the favor of the Lord our God be upon us,
and prosper for us the work of our hands.

Psalm 90:17

I was just talking yesterday about how much
the children are learning, O God, but today
I realized that I, too, am continuing to grow and learn.
May I never stop being a "student" of your will as I
move through this wondrous
passage of mothering.

Character building begins
in our infancy and continues
until death.

—Eleanor Roosevelt

February 3

I am the light of the world. Whoever follows me
will never walk in darkness but will have the light of life.

Be thou my vision, O Lord of my heart;
   Naught be all else to me, save that
  Thou art:
Thou my best thought, by day or by night,
Waking or sleeping, Thy presence my light.

Riches I heed not, nor man's empty praise,
Thou mine inheritance, now and always:
Thou and Thou only, first in my heart,
High King of heaven, my treasure Thou art.

"Be Thou My Vision"

Jesus is the Light of the world. Living near him
is the brightest place in the universe.
To find out where he lives,
read the Gospels and follow his path.

—John Piper, *A Hunger for God*

February 4

The one who is unwilling to work shall not eat.

2 Thessalonians 3:10 NIV

Gracious Father, you are at work day and night on our behalf as you watch over us. We want our children to know that work is a noble thing, a necessary part of life, and that we are all fellow workers with you.

We wish to teach the children that no matter how small the chore, it can and should be done to your glory.

We thank you, Lord, for the opportunity for honest labor, and we present ourselves to you as workers who need not be ashamed. Grant that our attitudes spill over into our children's lives so they, too, may know the satisfaction of earning their daily bread.

February 5

O come, let us worship and bow down,
let us kneel before the Lord, our Maker!

Psalm 95:6

Lord, my heart is uplifted as I think of the special gift you have given me: a community of faith. I thank you for my church and for the dear people who have become part of my support system. I thank you for your invitation to spend time with you.

My husband and children and I need the blessings of church attendance. We need the fellowship and care of other believers; we need to be refreshed with the words of scripture and feel the power of prayer washing over us. We need to experience your presence, Lord, in your house, and to become involved in your work.

Please continue to strengthen our children's ties to your church so that they, too, may participate in the joys of life in the Christian community.

People—reaching out and reaching up—that is the church.

February 6

If any want to become my followers, let them deny themselves and take up their cross and follow me.

Matthew 16:24

Dear Heavenly Father,

I confess that I have lived independently and have not denied myself, picked up my cross daily and followed You. In so doing, I have given ground to the enemy in my life. I have believed that I could be successful and live victoriously by my own strength and resources. I now confess that I have sinned against You by placing my will before Yours and by centering my life around myself instead of You. I now renounce the self-life.... I pray that You will guide me so that I will do nothing from selfish or empty conceit, but with humility of mind I will regard others as better than myself. Enable me through love to serve others and in honor prefer others. I ask this in the name of Christ Jesus, my Lord. Amen.

—Neil T. Anderson and Hal Baumchen, *Finding Hope Again*

My moments of greatest happiness come when I forget myself.

February 7

To every thing there is a season,
and a time to every purpose under the heaven.

Ecclesiastes 3:1 KJV

Dear God, I thank you for the opportunity to do both of the things I love: being a mother and holding down a meaningful job.

It has been hectic, Lord, and sometimes I wonder if my job is worth the late nights and weekends spent doing laundry and housework. I become so tired I can barely function.

I need your steadying hand, Father. I need you to help me discern what I can and cannot do. I need you to make the pieces fit.

You help me find balance in my day—to find a time for every purpose. After school and evenings are for my kids and husband; late nights and Saturdays are for chores. I wait for Sundays, Lord, to be with you and renew myself in worship.

I could not accomplish anything without your sweet spirit blowing through me, refreshing and strengthening me each day so I can give my best to my family and my job.

February 8

You show me the path of life.

Psalm 16:11

You hold in your hand my destiny.
    You determine, largely, whether I shall
succeed or fail.
Give me, I pray you, those things that make
    for happiness.
Train me, I beg you, that I may be a blessing
    to the world.

—James L. Christensen, *New Ways to Worship*

God provides signposts to help us find our way along this ever-changing journey of mothering. May we be wise enough to spot them in the lives of mentors, in writings, and even in examples of creative, loving mothering we see at the grocery store!

February 9

See, I am coming soon; my reward is with me,
to repay according to everyone's work.

Revelation 22:12

Being a mother today means so much more than just caring for children.

Being a mother today means being a role model for a growing soul; a guardian angel for a curious mind anxious to experience the world.

Being a mother today means being the best human being you can be, in order to set the best example you can for your children.

Being a mother today means knowing how to walk a path of balance between satisfying the needs of the self and fulfilling the needs of those around you, so that one day your children will know how to walk the same path.

When God blesses us with a loving mother,
we are truly blessed.

February 10

Let all who take refuge in you rejoice; let them ever sing for joy.

Psalm 5:11

Gracious Father, I have often asked myself this question: How do I make my home a place of joy? A place where my children and husband can relax and be happy? Now I know—the answer lies with you, O Lord. Like St. Augustine, our hearts are restless until they find their home in you. Joy begins when we let you in. Life seems steadier, brighter, friendlier, safer. Your presence fills us with music. We make joyful noises when we sing your praises. All thanks to you, precious Lord, for our happy home. I will sing to you as long as I live.

Joy is the presence of God in our lives, which brings music to our souls.

February 11

Now as they went on their way, he entered a certain village, where a woman named Martha welcomed him into her home. She had a sister named Mary, who sat at the Lord's feet and listened to what he was saying. But Martha was distracted by her many tasks; so she came to him and asked, "Lord, do you not care that my sister has left me to do all the work by myself? Tell her then to help me." But the Lord answered her, "Martha, Martha, you are worried and distracted by many things; there is need of only one thing. Mary has chosen the better part, which will not be taken away from her."

Luke 10:38–42

Lord Jesus, I want to worship You, adore You, and love You more each day. I want, like Mary, to choose the better part and sit at Your feet. Teach me to worship You more, teach me to feast on Your Word. Teach me how to live a life of uninterrupted communion with You.

—Wesley L. Duewel, *Touch the World through Prayer*

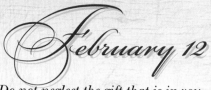

February 12

Do not neglect the gift that is in you.

1 Timothy 4:14

Our children are all different, Lord. Even if we tried, we could not push them all into the same mold. You have seen to it that each has different strengths and unique gifts. Each steps to a different drummer. We welcome and appreciate this diversity that makes our family a delightful rainbow, but we need your wisdom.

Help us discern what is right for each child. Guide us as we discover where their talents lie, and help us to nurture them according to those strengths and weaknesses. We thank you for all you have given us, and may we always honor you with our special gifts.

Each child is born to sing
a different song to God.

February 13

I have said this to you, so that in me you may have peace. In the world you face persecution. But take courage; I have conquered the world!

John 16:33

Oh Deliverer of Peace, you sent Christ to us not as a warrior, not as a judge, not as an enforcer, but as a baby, a healer, a teacher. Help me to follow Christ's example as peacekeeper in my home. Help me instill in my children the love of peace by acting in ways that are peaceful, not pun-  ishing; problem-solving, not judging; cooperating, not coercing. Help me to show my children your peace so that they may bring peace to others.

Moms are powerful purveyors of peacefulness. When a mother is at peace, her child responds more peacefully. Like a ray of sunshine that gives warmth to everything in its path, a mother's harmony gives order to everyone she comes in contact with.

February 14

"You shall love the Lord your God with all your heart, and with all your soul, and with all your mind." This is the greatest and first commandment. And a second is like it: "You shall love your neighbor as yourself."

Matthew 22:37–39

On Valentine's Day, a day to say "I love you," we remember you, O God. We are able to love only because you first loved us. You taught us how to love you and each other—our family and our neighbors.

We want our children to know your perfect love, and we invite the fragrance of your love to permeate our home.

Heavenly Father, you are the author of love. Write your name on our children's hearts, so they may enjoy the wondrous gifts you have prepared for those who love you.

*Love God first,
and all of your other relationships
will fall into place.*

February 15

In every thing give thanks: for this is the will of God in Christ Jesus.

1 Thessalonians 5:18 KJV

Heavenly Father, our children receive so much, yet they seldom seem to appreciate what they have and always want more: more toys, more possessions, more food, more spending money, more attention. Their cups run over, yet expressions of thanks need to be forced from them. If they are forthcoming, they seem mechanical and insincere.

Lord, I ask for your guidance to help kindle appreciation in my children's hearts for all of their blessings. I want them to know that every good gift comes from you, that they need to thank you as well as the giver of the gift.

My children are my greatest gifts. May I always remember to express my appreciation for them at the end of each day.

February 16

If you return to the Almighty, you will be restored.

Job 22:23

Thank you for keeping communication lines
  open,
And for the assurance that I am never forsaken
Even when I tune You out
As easily as changing a channel.

—Jan Markell, *Waiting for a Miracle*

It's been days since I even considered that I didn't have to be doing all I do alone—pretending to be supermom. Whew! What a relief to know that God remembered and reminded me. Partnerships are so much better than going it alone.

February 17

The Lord exists forever; your word is firmly fixed in heaven....
Your word is a lamp to my feet and a light to my path.

Psalm 119:89, 105

God! Thou art love! I build my faith on
that....
I know thee, who hast kept my path, and made
Light for me in darkness, tempering sorrow
So that it reached me like a solemn joy;
It were too strange that I should
doubt thy love.

—Robert Browning, "Paracelsus"

O Word of God incarnate,
O Wisdom from on high,
O Truth unchanged, unchanging,
O Light of our dark sky:
We praise you for the radiance
That from the hallowed page,
A lantern to our footsteps,
Shines on from age to age.

—William W. How, "O Word of God Incarnate"

February 18

Dear Lord, you have gifted me with children and I am humbly grateful, but I need Your wisdom to deal with my children gently but firmly as I ought. As they look up to me for guidance, I must look up to you. Shape me, O Lord, into the kind of model I should be. Let me assume this task unselfishly. Let me enrich their lives rather than expecting them to enrich my own. Where there are mountains, let me climb—knowing that small feet are following. And let my shadow be short that they may climb in the sunlight of Your love. Amen.

—June Masters Bacher, *A Mother's Joy*

Do you want wisdom? . . . You can have it if you want it, but you must make the decision to pursue wisdom with all your heart. But there is a further step you must take. It involves humbling yourself, admitting your need, confessing your lack, and asking God to help you.

—Ray Pritchard, *The ABC's of Wisdom*

February 19

He who is coming will come and will not delay.... But my righteous one will live by faith. And I take no pleasure in the one who shrinks back.

Hebrews 10:37–38 NIV

Lord, if there is one thing this woman can use more of, it is faith. Good, strong, solid faith. Faith in the harmony and order of a world I can't comprehend. Faith in your sovereignty over a society I often feel distrust for. Faith that my family will be protected and loved, even when I am not there to protect and love them. Most of all, dear Lord, I need faith in myself and in my abilities to grow as a woman, a wife, and a mother. So give me not diamonds or fancy cars. Those I can do without. Give me faith. Good, strong, solid faith. Amen.

*Faith is knowing that you cannot
always control what goes on outside of you,
but you can always control what goes on inside.
Faith is letting go and letting God help see you through.*

February 20

And let the peace of Christ rule in your hearts, to which indeed you were called in the one body. And be thankful.

Colossians 3:15

Lord, I have seen homes where family members were continually at war with one another. I don't want our family to live like that. With your help, I have resolved to make our home a quiet place for my husband and children—a refuge from the noise and discord of the world outside.

O God of peace and contentment, you have chosen us to live together both as a family and as part of the body of Christ. We invite you now to come into our home, our hearts, and our minds, so your peace may dwell there. Amen.

There may be those on earth who dress better or eat better, but those who enjoy the peace of God sleep better.

—L. Thomas Holdcroft

February 21

Whatever your hand finds to do, do with your might.

Ecclesiastes 9:10

Father God, protect me from the pull of volunteer jobs that claim too much of my time. It's so hard to say "no." All are worthy causes, but too many dilute my strength and prevent me from doing, with all my might, the work that is important to me.

You know me, Lord. You know what is best for me. You know what I can do and what I must do. Help me to choose wisely the activities that will be of most benefit to my family's welfare—activities that will not rob them of what they need most: a wife and a mother.

The Lord has promised good to me
His word my hope secures;
He will my shield and portion be
As long as life endures.

—John Newton,
"Amazing Grace! How Sweet the Sound"

February 22

The joy of the Lord is your strength.

Nehemiah 8:10

Help me teach my kids how to grow grace-
fully and excel, Lord of possibilities. Help
me pass on to them standards, goals, and a living
faith. Steady me as I help them soar; holding them
back says I think they can't.

*It's not possible to embrace kids' growth while requiring
they stay the same—even though it's tempting.
Change pinches like too-tight shoes!*

February 23

Love the Lord your God, listen to his voice, and hold fast to him.

Deuteronomy 30:20 NIV

Lord, teach me to listen. The times are noisy and my ears are weary with the thousand raucous sounds which continuously assault them. Give me the spirit of the boy Samuel when he said to Thee, "Speak, for thy servant heareth." Let me hear Thee speaking in my heart. Let me get used to the sound of Thy voice, that its tones may be familiar when the sounds of earth die away and the only sound will be the music of Thy speaking Voice. Amen.

—A.W. Tozer, *The Pursuit of God*

*Prayer not only offers me the place
to pour my heart before Him,
but prayer also provides a place
to listen and to learn God's heart,
to see the world as He does.*

—Nancie Carmichael, *Desperate for God*

February 24

I have no greater joy than this, to hear that my children are walking in the truth.

3 John 4

Lord, in a society that condones deception and half-truths, I long to teach my children the importance of honesty, of keeping promises, and of doing what they say they will do. Help me to begin with myself.

Keep me always aware of my own integrity in my relationships with others. Let me be a person my family and friends can count on to speak truthfully and to deliver what is promised.

To make your children capable of honesty is the beginning of education.
—John Ruskin, *Time and Tide*

February 25

For though I be free from all men,
yet have I made myself servant unto all.

1 Corinthians 9:19 KJV

Lord, my God, your son took on the role of a servant to all people. As a mother, I find myself walking in his footsteps. Service to my family has become life's greatest pleasure. I give myself willingly, not because someone demands that I serve but because I want to.

As I cook and provide meals, wash clothes, and maintain my home as a place of comfort for my husband and children, my heart sings with the joy of fulfillment. When I consider that no job was too lowly for Jesus, even scrubbing the floor brings me satisfaction.

I thank and praise you, dear Father, for turning an independent person like me into a willing servant in your kingdom.

February 26

Weeping may linger for the night, but joy comes with the morning.

Psalm 30:5

O Love that wilt not let me go,
    I rest my weary soul in thee;
I give thee back the life I owe,
That in thine ocean depths its flow
May richer, fuller be.

O Light that followest all my way,
I yield my flick'ring torch to thee;
My heart restores its borrowed ray,
That in thy sunshine's blaze its day
May brighter, fairer be.

O Joy that seekest me through pain,
I cannot close my heart to thee;
I trace the rainbow thru the rain,
And feel the promise is not vain
That morn shall tearless be.

—George Matheson, "O Love That Wilt Not Let Me Go"

February 27

*Bear with one another and, if anyone has a complaint against another,
forgive each other; just as the Lord has forgiven you,
so you also must forgive.*

Colossians 3:13

y husband and I got into a silly quarrel,
O God of peacemaking and love, and
we are having a hard time making up. Please guide us
to common ground where
you hold each of us by the
hand and inspire us
toward compromise.
Amen.

*God pardons like a mother
who kisses the offense
into everlasting forgetfulness.*

—Henry Ward Beecher

February 28

Don't store up treasures on earth! Moths and rust can destroy them, and thieves can break in and steal them. Instead, store up your treasures in heaven. . . . Your heart will always be where your treasure is.

Matthew 6:19–21 CEV

Father, we try to live modestly and not flaunt our belongings before those who have less. But our children are surrounded by playmates who pile up possessions only to tire of them and quickly discard them. Our children are envious and think they, too, need the latest toys and the trendiest clothes.

How can we convince them that things can't make them happy? How do we instill in them the values that will make their lives fulfilling? Help us, O Lord, to plant in their hearts yearnings for the important things in life, such as friendships, love for God, healthy bodies, creative minds, and helping hearts.

Our children are our most valued treasures. Humbly we commend them to your care.

Your own values preach the most effective sermon.

February 29

*Take my yoke upon you, and learn from me; for I am gentle
and humble in heart, and you will find rest for your souls.
For my yoke is easy, and my burden is light.*

Matthew 11:29–30

Lord,
    Teach me to love as you love
for I know that is the only way I can show
my gratitude for your love of me.
        Sometimes it's easy to love when all is
          going well.
            I need you when loving is not easy.
           It's hard to love
            when I'm tired and see no signs
             of relief;
             when the kids are demanding
             and totally selfish;
            when I just don't like what others
         are doing,
          even those closest to me.
        Enable me to love not because I feel
     like it
but because that is what we are created to do
and because it is the only way for there to be hope in
this world.

My Prayer Life

_____

_____

_____

_____

_____

_____

_____

_____

_____

_____

_____

_____

_____

March 1

ord, I renounce the lie that my self-worth is dependent upon my ability to perform. I announce the truth that my identity and sense of worth are found in who I am as your child. I renounce seeking approval and acceptance of other people, and I choose to believe that I am already approved and accepted in Christ because of his death and resurrection for me. I choose to believe the truth that I have been saved, not by deeds done in righteousness but according to your mercy. . . . I receive the free gift of life in Christ and choose to abide in him. I renounce striving for perfection by living under the law. By your grace, Heavenly Father, I choose from this day forward to walk by faith according to what you have said is true by the power of your Holy Spirit. In Jesus' name. Amen.

—Neil T. Anderson and Hal Baumchen, *Finding Hope Again*

There are no perfect parents. . . . When your children see that you are willing to admit your mistakes and promise to try to do better next time, they can be quite forgiving.

—Dr. Bruce Narramore, *Help! I'm a Parent*

March 2

He has rescued us from the power of darkness and transferred us into the kingdom of his beloved Son. . . . He is the image of the invisible God.

Colossians 1:13, 15

Gracious God, help me to reflect your warmth to my family, to reflect your light that sparks their imagination and kindles their compassion. May my children know your presence through me, through the way I embody your spirit to them. Help me to change the world by creating children who exude warmth and light, dispelling the shadows around them. Amen.

A mother is the centerpiece of the whole fabric of a family, like the spinner and weaver of beautiful, useful cloth. In even the finest tapestry, each varied thread gives it added loveliness by the uniqueness.

March 3

As a mother comforts her child, so I will comfort you.

Isaiah 66:13

Life can be harsh for a small child, Lord. When one of my children comes home in tears, I want to cry, too. A mom quickly learns to be a comforter, and I am no exception. I gather my child into my arms and hold on. Then I croon soft, consoling words into a dainty shell-like ear until the tears stop and a weak smile appears, like the sun peeking out from behind a cloud.

It's harder to comfort grown-ups, Lord, so mostly I give hugs and then just listen. I imagine I'm you, hearing the prayers of your people. Thank you, Father, for giving me a listening heart and for allowing me to be part of your ministry of comfort.

To comfort others as Christ has comforted you is to be his hands reaching down from heaven.

Dear God,
    Am I doing this OK? Am I the best I can be?
Can I juggle all these balls of being mother, wife, and
    friend?
And what about the woman that I once called "me"?
Will she ever resurface, or is this, for her, the end?

Can I do things right and get it straight in just one try?
Do I get to do it over if things don't go as I intend?
Will I have the time to chase the dreams that make my
    spirits fly,
When all my days are filled with being mother, wife,
    and friend?

Your experiences, talents, loves and hates will fill your life
and fully prepare you for the day when your children
grow and go. At that point, when you are forced to stand
alone and ask yourself, "Who am I?"
you can easily answer, "I am a fulfilled person."

—Sanford J. Matthews, M.D., and Maryann Bucknum Brinley

March 5

The peace of God, which surpasses all understanding, will guard your hearts and your minds in Christ Jesus.

Philippians 4:7

Listen, Lord, a mother's praying low and quiet:
   listen please.
Listen what her tears are saying,
   see her heart upon its knees;
lift the load from her bowed shoulders
   till she sees and understands,
You, who hold the worlds together,
   hold her problems in Your hands.

—Ruth Bell Graham, *Prodigals and Those Who Love Them*

Give thanks and praise for what you have, and your prayers are already answered.

March 6

Lord, teach us to pray.

Father in heaven, we want to teach our children how to pray. There are so many things we want them to know about prayer, but where do we start? How do we explain that though you always hear us, your answer may not come right away? How do we get them beyond the recitation of rote prayers to express prayers from their hearts? How do we discourage frivolous prayers without stifling spontaneity?

We are touched with joy when we hear those first attempts at prayer, free from self-consciousness and wrapped in innocence.

It is an awesome thing, Lord, to instruct our children in your ways. Guide us as we teach them about the most important conversations they will ever have.

Prayer is exhaling the spirit of man and inhaling the spirit of God.

—Edwin Keith

March 7

I am about to do a new thing; now it springs forth, do you not perceive it? I will make a way in the wilderness and rivers in the desert.

Isaiah 43:19

God, I thank thee for the gift of another day.
May I meet the unspent hours that are ahead
With brave heart as one who puts his trust in thee
And trusting is unafraid.
May every thought be pure and every purpose holy.
Make me generous in spirit, tolerant in judgement,
Unselfish in all human relations.
Keep back the hasty or the careless words,
And may nothing that I do or say wound or harm
    another.
May I meet life courageously,
Bearing with patience the hope deferred
And the dream unrealized.

—Alfred Grant Walton

*In the end I did find the secret, and it was this: There
is no one secret way to be a "good" mother. Each of us
has to invent motherhood for herself and invent it over
and over and over as we move forward through it.*

—Frances Wells Burck

March 8

In this world you will have trouble. But take heart!
I have overcome the world.

I am weak, but Thou art strong;
 Jesus, keep me from all wrong;
I'll be satisfied as long
As I walk, let me walk close to Thee.

Through this world of toil and snares,
If I falter, Lord, who cares?
Who with me my burden shares?
None but Thee, dear Lord, none but Thee.

Just a closer walk with Thee,
Grant it, Jesus, is my plea,
Daily walking close to Thee,
Let it be, dear Lord, let it be.

—Anonymous

Through Bryon, our small bundle of joyous energy—a
gift from God—we have discovered that in the midst of
sorrow God alone can draw the sting out of every trouble
and take the bitterness from every affliction.

—Lillian Sparks, *Parents Cry Too!*

March 9

Train children in the right way, and when old, they will not stray.

Proverbs 22:6

Talk about being torn, O Merciful God. I am
when it comes to this correcting business. I
know giving loving guidance can be life-enhancing,
but, if done improperly, it can rob my children of their individuality. Give me guidance to know when I am acting creatively
and lovingly and when I am overstepping
my role as a parent. Then, correct me,
O Forgiving God.

*When we draw a circle
around ourselves to shut
him out, God draws a
larger circle to take us in.*

March 10

Lord, I try to remain calm and loving, but sometimes I get so upset with my kids that I want to explode. I'm not proud of the hurtful words that come out of my mouth, but I can't seem to stop them.

Father, you are the God of peace. Fill me with your quiet spirit. Teach me to get control of my anger before lashing out at the children. Prevent me from blaming them instead of calmly stating the reasons for my anger.

Remind me that my aim is to soothe and not to stir up anger. Give me a tongue that is soft and gentle rather than harsh and perverse so my young ones will be inspired to change their behavior.

Fresh out of methods, struck out on my plans
Nowhere to quit . . . can't wash my hands.
Filled with self-hatred, hanging my head
God lifted my chin then gently said,
But, Can you just love him?

—Beth Moore, *Things Pondered*

March 11

So if anyone is in Christ, there is a new creation: everything old has passed away; see, everything has become new!

2 Corinthians 5:17

Not wasting a moment, a child leaps from sleep and skips into a wonder-filled day, assuming it to be one! See, too, how they jump to their feet after a fall or rise in curiosity after disappointment, knowing more good than bad sums up each day. Ah, an example to follow.

My candle burns at both ends;
It will not last the night;
But ah, my foes, and oh, my friends—
It gives a lovely light!

—Edna St. Vincent Millay, "First Fig"

March 12

You grew weary from your many wanderings, but you did not say, "It is useless." You found your desire rekindled, and so you did not weaken.

Isaiah 57:10

Galvanize me into prevention, intervention, and rebuilding your world, Creator God. Kids need fixers, not just worriers and those prone to panic. They need to hear plans, not just alarms. Let hope, not fear, be the last word in the bedtime stories I tell.

*When life's taken its best shot,
dig in and lift eyes skyward. Feel it?
That's God's spirit blowing across weary lives,
filling us with a second wind.*

March 13

Or do you not know that your body is a temple of the Holy Spirit within you, which you have from God?... Therefore glorify God in your body.

1 Corinthians 6:19–20

Our bodies are temples, Lord. You have said so. We need to care for them with a balance of exercise, good nutrition, and proper rest. None of these seem to be popular with youngsters today, but we ask you to help us instill in our children respect for bodily fitness.

We love our children, Lord, and we are serious in our desire to encourage them to develop healthy bodies and minds. Bless us as we try to be better examples by doing more walking and less driving, avoiding junk food, and spending less time in front of the TV and computer.

Please guard our entire family from harmful excesses as we work to keep our bodies fit to honor you.

*Take care of your body;
it's the only one you'll get.*

March 14

Never will I leave you; never will I forsake you.

Hebrews 13:5 NIV

Lord, I am here.—But child, I look for thee
Elsewhere and nearer me.—
Lord, that way moans a wide insatiate sea:
How can I come to Thee?—
Set foot upon the water, test and see
If thou canst come to me.—
Couldst Thou not send a boat to carry me,
Or dolphin swimming free?—

Nay, boat nor fish if thy will faileth thee:
For My Will too is free.—
O Lord, I am afraid.—Take hold on me:
I am stronger than the sea.—
Save, Lord, I perish.—I have hold of thee.
I made and rule the sea,
I bring thee to the haven where thou wouldst be.

—Christina Rossetti, "Christ Our All in All"

March 15

I have learned to be content with whatever I have.

Philippians 4:11

ontentment is hard to learn. But I know, Lord, that you can give me peace in every circumstance and the contentment it brings as I submit to your lordship. Teach me to trust you for each day's problems and rely on you to strengthen me for every task. I can be content as long as I know you are with me, helping me at every turn.

—Charles Stanley, *A Touch of His Peace*

For their part, kids are like sponges— they absorb all your strength and leave you limp, but give them a squeeze and you get it all back!

—Barbara Johnson,
Boomerang Joy

March 16

Lord, bless this mess. Bless this Monday house—
breakfast dishes in the sink, bed still unmade,
clutter of sandwich makings on the cabinet,
living room awry.
Bless this mess, and me, as I proceed to tackle it.
Lord, bless this mess. Bless this Monday mind—
cluttered and cobwebby,
catch-all for outgrown opinions and ill-fitting prejudices,
its mental compartments not yet straightened out,
thought patterns that could do with a good airing.
Bless this mess, and me, as I proceed to tackle it.
Lord, bless this day.
The mop and broom I can handle. I need thy help
with the cleansing of my mind.
Amen.

—Jo Carr and Imogene Sorley

If we look hard enough, we find blessings in every-
thing, even dirty dishes, unwashed laundry, and
chocolate stains on the refrigerator door. Those
things remind us that we are part of a family, for
better and for worse. But mostly for better.

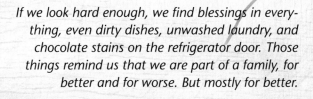

March 17

Cast all your anxiety on him, because he cares for you.

1 Peter 5:7

As I send my family from our home this morning, Lord, I cannot be with each of them, so I trust them to your care. Please watch over them.

Put peace in my children's hearts. Protect them from harm, and grant them strength and courage to face each day. Make my husband equal to the mental and physical demands made upon him. Let all enjoy the work of their hands and the fellowship of coworkers or classmates.

When their day of school or work is over, give them the satisfaction of having done their best and the assurance they will be welcomed home with loving arms.

As my husband and children go out into the world, it is comforting to know that the Lord goes before them to lead the way and to give them light.

March 18

He will be our guide forever.

Psalm 48:14

Thank you, God, that even when I fret, I know without a doubt that you are using my unique, special gifts and talents to nurture and teach my children. When I get down on myself and am unsure of my abilities, remind me that your commitment to me is lifelong.

Aim high, believing that God has great things in store for us as mothers and for our families. Never mind naysayers and "practical" roadblocks, for we are guided by God.

March 19

Don't get tired of helping others. You will be rewarded
when the time is right, if you don't give up.

Over and over I ask myself, O Loving Shepherd,
"What can I do?" What can I do to help, to make
a difference, to relieve those I love of their hurts? The
hardest thing about this mothering role is having
others think I can "fix it" and then finding out that I
can't, as much as I would like to. Remind me that what
you promise is not to "fix it" for us but rather to give us
whatever it takes to prevail in spite of our hurts. Help
me to see that sharing a tear is sometimes all that is
necessary.

March 20

And let the peace of Christ rule in your hearts.

Colossians 3:15

Take my hand, precious Lord, as I take on the role of peacemaker. Lead me through the minefield of broken relationships between my child and another.

Make me sensitive to hurt feelings on both sides, and fill me with the compassion and understanding to negotiate the delicate situation fairly.

Give both children an appreciation for the friendship they have enjoyed, and make them understand the need for apology and forgiveness. Help them to put the past behind them, start fresh, and build a new relationship.

It is painful to see misery on these young children's faces, Lord. Use me to help them mend this friendship and restore the sunshine.

A true friend is the gift of God,
and he only who made hearts can unite them.

—Robert South

March 21

Be glad in the Lord and rejoice.

Psalm 32:11

Father in heaven, the ground is thawing, the air is warming, and finally the children can get outdoors to play. Hurray, and thank you, Lord! Their behavior improves immediately. They are less inclined to whine and bicker, and bedtime is so much easier when they are physically tired.

It's good to see sunshine and green shoots again, but I thank you most for the changed attitudes and conduct of my family. Winter has its own beauty, Lord, but spring brings hope and plenty of smiles.

March is the window to nature's most joyous season.

March 22

Father, you are a God of love, compassion, and forgiveness. You have shown my family the right way to live in the world. You are a God my children can rely on to guide them and keep safe. What wonders you perform!

Your power at work in us can accomplish more than our meager minds can even conceive. You boost our confidence and make us better than we are.

In times of trouble, you find solutions we never could have imagined. Lord, we do not deserve your care and attention, but you give them anyway. For this we exalt you forever.

How much does God love you?
He loves you enough to let you go.
He loves you enough to let you hit bottom.
He loves you enough to let you come back.
He loves you so much that he will run to meet you.
That's how much God loves you.

—Ray Pritchard, *The Road Best Traveled*

March 23

Those who are generous are blessed,
for they share their bread with the poor.

Proverbs 22:9

Sharing has to be one of life's most difficult
lessons—for the kids, for me, for everyone,
O Bountiful God. Remind me that to choose to "give
away" my time, my energy, myself, makes a gracious gift
instead of a grudging duty.

Give what you have.
To some it may be better than you dare think.

—Henry Wadsworth Longfellow

March 24

Let anyone who is thirsty come to me, and let the one who believes in me drink. As the scripture has said, "Out of the believer's heart shall flow rivers of living water."

John 7:37–38

God,
> You have given me this gift of life to care for and nurture.

May I be worthy of the task.

You have trusted me with the new responsibilities of being a parent.

May I be worthy of the task.

You have shown faith enough in me to bless me with a family.

May I be worthy of the task.

You have honored me by giving me the right to call myself "mother."

May I be worthy of the task.

Amen.

An affirmation for all mothers to empower themselves to be the best they can be in all aspects of their lives: I am strong. I am worthy. I am more than up to the task.

March 25

The heavens are telling the glory of God;
and the firmament proclaims his handiwork.

Psalm 19:1

How do I explain your greatness to my children, O God? How do I tell of all your wonderful works? I will tell them to look up. The sky displays the work of your hands.

By day, in blazing splendor, the sun bespeaks your power. In the inverted black bowl of night, the stars shout your glory. Orion, Pleiades, the Bear, make their seasonal journey across the wide expanse in praise of you. Even the moon reflects your wondrous light.

The sky says it all, O Lord. We just need to look up to see what you have done.

The stars speak of man's insignificance
in the long eternity of time.

—Edwin Way Teale

March 26

I give you a new commandment, that you love one another. Just as I have loved you, you also should love one another. By this everyone will know that you are my disciples, if you have love for one another.

John 13:34–35

Lord, the new command you gave your disciples, to love one another, is just what we need to challenge our children when they fight among themselves. We want to remind them that they're not showing their love when they quarrel, because love is kind, patient, and doesn't insist on its own way.

Our thanks and praise to you, dear Father, for the tender messages from your word. May they take root and grow in our children's hearts.

*When you give another your love,
you are giving your greatest riches—
the gift of yourself.*

March 27

"God opposes the proud, but gives grace to the humble."...
Humble yourselves before the Lord, and he will exalt you.

James 4:6, 10

hatever I have, Lord, you gave it to me. I can't take credit for any of it, so how silly I am when I am filled with pride.... Trying to make myself feel humble, Lord, is a little like trying to pull myself up by my own shoelaces.

I can't do it, God. So, please, You do it for me. Fill my heart with humility. Amen.

—*Light for My Path*

I think I would be a much better mother if I knew my house were bugged and I would be required to listen—every night—to every word I had said that day. It seems that knowing my children are naturally bugged and will hear over and over again every word I say would have more bearing on me than it does.

—Wilda Fancher, *The Christian Woman in the Christian Home*

March 28

There is nothing better for people under the sun than to eat, and drink, and enjoy themselves.

Ecclesiastes 8:15

Lord, some of our best family times occur when we can all sit down together to enjoy a meal and conversation. It's even better when we have company to share the fun.

After the blessing of food and family, everyone has a chance to be heard, humor is encouraged, and appetites flourish. Some of life's greatest problems are settled around our table.

Father, I am grateful that you are a God who wants us to enjoy ourselves. From my heart I thank you for the food that you supply, the closeness of our family, and the circle of love that surrounds us.

No custom is more pleasant than getting to know each other around the dinner table.

March 29

But let the righteous be joyful; let them exult before God;
let them be jubilant with joy.

Psalm 68:3

Thank you, O God, for those moments of indescribable joy that surprise, that greet me unexpectedly in a child's hug, a drawing, a conversation, an uncontrollable giggle, and most especially an openness that not only lets me into their lives but draws me in.

Whoop and holler in delight
at the joy of being a mother,
recognizing it as God's call.

O Loving God,
bless our family with your love.
Guard us from all danger and harm;
deliver us from anger that leads to division;
empower us to forgive as we have been forgiven;
and send us into the world
to witness your love and grace;
in the name of Jesus Christ we pray.
Amen.

—Vienna Cobb Anderson, "A Prayer for Our Family"

Because mothering is like sowing seeds, you often don't see the fruits right away. It takes time to reap the reward. There are no guarantees, either. But if you do your best, relying on God for wisdom and strength, there's a good chance that your day to see wonderful fruit will come.

—Linda Weber

March 31

Yea, though I walk through the valley of the shadow of death,
I will fear no evil: for thou art with me.

Heavenly Father, it is difficult to talk about death with my children. When friends or relatives die, my children need to know that death is a natural part of life; that this earthly life is not all there is; that we will all meet again in heaven some day.

Yet the earthly loss is painful. It causes loneliness and sorrow and sometimes fear. These feelings can't be readily erased. My children need to know that you are with them.

Help me to find the words that will point them to you, Lord—words that will glorify you, words that will soothe and take away my children's fears. Help me to deal with the sad feelings in tangible ways, so the sorrow is alleviated little by little. Make your presence known to each of my children in their times of need, and shelter them from the sting of death.

Hold my hand, Lord, so I will not be afraid.

My Prayer Life

_____

_____

_____

_____

_____

_____

_____

_____

_____

_____

_____

_____

April 1

Thank the Lord for his steadfast love,
for his wonderful works to humankind.

Psalm 107:8

God, we thank you for this food
for the hands that planted it
for the hands that tended it
for the hands that harvested it
for the hands that prepared it
for the hands that provided it
and for the hands that served it.
And we pray for those without enough food
in your world and in our land of plenty.

If the only prayer you say in your entire life is Thank you,
that would suffice.

—Meister Eckhart

April 2

I waited patiently for the Lord; he inclined to me and heard my cry.

Psalm 40:1

My Lord, I pray that through today
I may walk patiently,
Forgetting not that Thy dear hand
Is leading me.

I know not what Thy wisdom, Lord,
May choose for me today,
What the long hours may hold for me
I cannot say.

I only know that I may go
Unquestioningly with Thee,
Remembering that what Thou wilt
Is best for me.

For Thou, Oh, Lord, canst see the end,
While I but see the way—
Help me to walk it patiently
Throughout today.

—Grace Noll Crowell, "A Prayer," *Songs for Courage*

Patience is love in disguise, going that extra mile.

April 3

Listen to this wise advice; follow it closely, for it will do you good, and you can pass it on to others: Trust in the Lord.

Proverbs 22:17–19 LB

Heavenly Father, make me a better parent. Teach me to understand my children, to listen patiently to what they have to say, and to answer all their questions kindly. Keep me from interrupting them or contradicting them. Make me as courteous to them as I would have them be to me. Forbid that I should ever laugh at their mistakes, or resort to shame or ridicule when they displease me. May I never punish them for my own selfish satisfaction or to show my power.... Make me fair and just and kind. And fit me, O Lord, to be loved and respected and imitated by my children.

—"A Parent's Prayer," *Let There Be Light*

I love little children, and it is not a slight thing when they, who are fresh from God, love us.

—Charles Dickens

April 4

*Where two or three are gathered together in my name,
there am I in the midst of them.*

Matthew 18:20 KJV

Heavenly Father, we thank you for the traditions that unite our family when we celebrate church holidays. We are bonded together in love as we take part in the rituals that were begun so long ago.

Bless us with your presence as we attend worship services together, partake of our traditional dinner, and enjoy one another's company.

These traditions make family the first priority for the day. They provide our children with security and confirm that we are important as a group. Please keep us close to each other as we gather around you.

*Customs and traditions
help define us
and give our family
its identity.*

April 5

If you confess with your lips that Jesus is Lord and believe in your heart that God raised him from the dead, you will be saved.

Romans 10:9

Living God, we sing for joy as we remember again the resurrection of your son, Jesus. Because he died and rose again, our hopes for paradise are real. Because he lives, we live.

Fill us with wonder as together our family contemplates the awesome mystery of the cross. Accept our praises and our songs of gratitude. Alleluia!

Christ is risen!
God has had the final word.

April 6

Thank You, O God,
For seeing beyond the surface of my life....

Thank You for sitting down beside me, putting Your arm around me, and speaking to me with such tenderness, such compassion, and such understanding.

Help me to be aware of the pictures in my life that are everywhere around me and at all times showing me something I need to see, telling me something I need to hear, offering me something I need to receive.

Help me look beyond the surface of those pictures to see windows.

Give me eyes to see, ears to hear, and a heart to receive what You are offering me through those windows, that I might sense what is dear to You so that it might become what is dear to me.

—Ken Gire, *Windows of the Soul*

He looks on my life in tenderness for He loves me deeply.
—Phillip Keller, *A Shepherd Looks at Psalm 23*

April 7

Heavenly Father, as I tend to all of the never-ending details of being a mom, I find myself wishing away stages of my child's life. I can't wait until my infant sleeps through the night, until I won't have to scrape baby food off the floor and wall anymore, or until we can get rid of diapers.

Lord, help me to be content in every circumstance. Help me to retain my sense of humor, to enjoy the moment, to savor each phase of my child's development as a wondrous unfolding of a new life, a gift from you.

I rejoice greatly over all of your gifts, dear Lord, and I thank you for the most important career I will ever have—that of being a mother.

I asked for God's greatest riches,
and he gave me contentment.

April 8

Let each of you look not to your own interests,
but to the interests of others.

Philippians 2:4

So much need around us, O Lord. Inspire me to
teach the children how to care for those who
need. Even the smallest gesture in the hand of a child
is more powerful than magic, bringing moments of
peace and contentment into circumstances thought
hopeless. Help me to become childlike in my care for
others.

God does not comfort us
to make us comfortable,
but to make us comforters.

—John Henry Jowett

April 9

You must understand this, my beloved:
let everyone be quick to listen, slow to speak, slow to anger.

James 1:19

Listening is an art that you have perfected, Lord. I am thankful that you listen when your children pray and share their deepest concerns. Let me, too, be quick to listen to my children's words and slow to speak.

Listening shows my youngsters that I care—that their feelings are important to me. Listening reassures them that their ideas and opinions have merit. I pray that I can be the kind of listener that my children need.

O loving Father, help me to listen carefully to the outpouring of my children's hearts so I can help them heal and grow strong. Amen.

People think listening is doing nothing. But listening—
real listening—is hard work that takes place in the heart.

April 10

"Do you believe that I am able to do this?" They said to him,
"Yes, Lord." Then he touched their eyes and said,
"According to your faith let it be done to you."

Matthew 9:28–29

A Mother's Meditation

There is nothing but peace in my life today. I know only serenity inside, despite what is going on outside of me. I react positively to every event I am faced with today. I respond with only love and kindness, no matter what I am responding to. I am empowered and strengthened from within, and I am capable of handling any challenge that faces me, any obstacle that obstructs my path to a perfect, joyful experience of being alive today.

And so it is.

It is empowering to know that we can choose to
be happy and whole each moment of each day.
Though outside events may change,
we remain strong, steadfast, and unwavering
when we remember—the choice is ours.

April 11

Blessed be the God and Father of our Lord Jesus Christ, the Father of mercies and the God of all consolation, who consoles us in all our affliction, so that we may be able to console those who are in any affliction with the consolation with which we ourselves are consoled by God.

2 Corinthians 1:3–4

Like aching bones that find
    relief in a steamy, hot bath,
O God, I long for comfort.
Take from my life the fear, the
hurt, the doubt, the
unknown, the insecurity—
the afflictions. Nonetheless,
your promise is to comfort us in
our afflictions and not remove
them. Help me to know that I will experience the
"relief" I want only when I am open to accepting your
healing comfort that gives us the strength to triumph.

*There are times when all of us feel
comfortless and helpless, but there is
great strength in remembering
the one who abides with us.*

—Charles L. Allen, *Victories in the Valleys of Life*

April 12

Whoever is kind to the poor lends to the Lord.

Proverbs 19:17

Merciful Lord, we share your compassion for the downtrodden and the poor. We ask you to stir up in our children the same kind of compassion for those who are less fortunate. Show them that you can use even our smallest efforts to help others.

Loving God, you have given us so much. Guide us as we look for appropriate ways for each of our children to help at their age level. As we involve them in our own activities of collecting for the food pantry, walking for charity, or pledging for causes through our church, help them to capture the spirit of giving. Teach us all the joy of giving in secret, without thought of reward.

Our own self-worth is developed as we help and serve others.

April 13

*May the God of hope fill you with all joy and peace in believing,
so that you may abound in hope by the power of the Holy Spirit.*

Romans 15:13

do lose hope, sometimes, Lord. But thank
you that you never give up on me. Your love,
faithfulness, and goodness are sufficient. I can have
hope. I don't have to quit in despair. You are able to
uphold me with your strong hand and breathe into me
all the hope I need for every load I bear.

—Charles Stanley, *A Touch of His Peace*

*This is a constant process in my life.
God exchanging His presence for
my loneliness—His power for my
weakness—His healing for my
illness—His hope for my despair—His
peace for my anxiety—His love for my
resentment—His grace for my suffering—
His comfort for my sorrow.*

—Evelyn Christenson, *Lord, Change Me*

April 14

No good tree bears bad fruit, nor again does a bad tree bear good fruit; for each tree is known by its own fruit.

Luke 6:43–44

Not everyone has the special family that I have, nor do they have the extra opportunities to open their hearts in the way my family does. We are not limited by what the neighbors think nor by society's prejudices. We are far more than that. We are a family that comes from love, and we accept with pride every unique member. I am special and I am worthy of love. I love and accept each member of my wonderful family, and they, in turn, love and adore me. I am safe. All is well in my world.

—Louise L. Hay

A happy family is but an earlier heaven.

—Sir John Bowring

April 15

The beloved of the Lord rests in safety—the High God surrounds him all day long—the beloved rests between his shoulders.

Deuteronomy 33:12

God of all comfort, have mercy on me. I got angry today at my husband and accused him of not helping me enough. I scolded my child for talking too much. I shouted at the dog for barking too loud. And I almost hung up on my neighbor for taking up too much of my time with her plumbing problems. I need your comforting strength, dear God, wrapped around me like a soothing blanket, so that I can ask my family for forgiveness. Bless me with more patience, too, so that we don't have to go through all this again tomorrow. Thank you, God.

Go easy on yourself, Mom. You can't be 100 percent perfect 100 percent of the time, no matter how much you would like to be. You are only human. You make mistakes. You ask for forgiveness. You learn to do better, and you move on.

April 16

*Come no closer! Remove the sandals from your feet,
for the place on which you are standing is holy ground.*

elp us to relax, Lord of calming seas, so that we don't become numb to the joy and awe of children, of family. For it's socially acceptable to kick off our shoes and tangibly feel the love. Make us alive, O God, to the holy grounds of life, and save us from taking these special places for granted.

*Take off your shoes of distraction
Take off your shoes of ignorance and blindness
Take off your shoes of hurry and worry
Take off anything that prevents you
from being a child of wonder.*

—Macrina Wiederkehr, *Seasons of Your Heart*

April 17

If a brother or sister is naked and lacks daily food,
and one of you says to them, "Go in peace; keep warm and eat your fill,"
and yet you do not supply their bodily needs, what is the good of that?
So faith by itself, if it has no works, is dead.

James 2:15–17

Let me not turn away from the oppressed, the needy, Lord, in order to "protect" the children. Instead, nudge me to enlist them with the invitation to help find solutions that we can do as a family. In this way they learn that they, too, can make a difference.

Just as the first bird to discover the feeder
is full sings out so others can also dine,
so can sharing discoveries in a family
nourish the whole.

April 18

The beloved of the Lord shall dwell in safety by him.

Deuteronomy 33:12 KJV

Father, newspaper headlines remind us continually of tragic accidents happening to children in their own homes. You are our shield against danger. We put our trust in you. We thank you for the protection you have already provided, and we depend on your help in making our home a safe place for our children.

Guard us from carelessness, and heighten our awareness of dangerous situations that need to be corrected. Help us to find ways to protect our children, and prevent us from thoughtlessly putting them at risk.

Heavenly Father, you love our children as we do, and we cling to your promise that they will dwell in safety with you as their protector.

A parent's love is not enough.
A child's life continues to need
the miracle touch of God.

—Ron Hutchcraft, *5 Needs Your Child Must Have Met at Home*

April 19

Whatever God does endures forever; nothing can be added to it, nor anything taken from it. God has done this, so that all should stand in awe before him.

Ecclesiastes 3:14

Lord, help me to remember that I am a woman first, mother and wife second. For if I forget that essential element of who I am, I cannot be the best mother or the best wife, for I will not be the best me. Guide me along my path, and give me the intuition to make the best decisions for me and for my family. Illumine my way so that I am not tempted by selfishness or selflessness. Make me not a martyr but a powerful giver. Make me not a victim but a happy participant in all the joys and frustrations of this life I have chosen. Oh, and please don't allow me to lose my sense of humor. Amen.

I woke up one morning and thought, "Here I am with two kids at home, doing all kinds of stuff I never thought I'd do. For example, who made me into the Queen of the Jello Molds?"

—Bonnie Januszewski-Ytuarte

April 20

He rewards those who seek him.

Hebrews 11:6

Sometimes, God, you're not very easy to see.
Maybe that's because I'm being half-hearted
about my seeking. Help me to seek you with my whole
heart. Remind me to seek you in everything I do,
wherever I am. Amen.

—*Light for My Path*

*Oh! if we could but lie closer on His breast and listen more
softly to His whisperings, He would often speak to us of things
to come, and we would dwell with Him in the soft sweet light
of the land of Beulah, living under the powers of the world to
come and seeing "The King in his beauty."*

—A. B. Simpson, *The Highest Christian Life*

April 21

Blessed Creator, there are days when I am not sure I am doing a good job of being a mother. My children seem angry, and I do not know why. My house knows no peace, yet I cannot find the cause of the distress. My heart seems heavy, but the reason for such suffering eludes me. Help me to find the good, the truth, and the lessons to be learned in these darker moments, so that when the light finally does return, I will have grown from them just as my children will have grown. Amen.

All mothering is made up both of affectionate caring and bitter emotional pain. In both emotions, the mother is close to the child, allowing the child, even as she feels her pain and anger, to become an individual through exposure to experience and to fate.

—Thomas Moore, *Care of the Soul*

April 22

Children are a blessing and a gift from the Lord.

Psalm 127:3 CEV

Father, you have enriched my life with many identities—daughter, student, wife, and mother. Richness and joy have followed me through each phase of my life, and I have wholeheartedly accepted and enjoyed each role. But you knew, didn't you, Lord, that the title of mother would make such a strong claim on my heart?

How I praise you for the greatest of your gifts, my children, and for the fulfillment they have brought. I need no other affirmation than to be called mother.

My children have taught me to forget myself, and through them, I have learned what it means to be your child.

To give birth to a child
is to share with God
a tiny piece of creation.

April 23

*Rejoice . . . while you are young, and let your heart cheer you
in the days of your youth.*

Ecclesiastes 11:9

nspired by you, O God, I wisely invest in the future by deciding to chase kites on spring days, to chase balls on playgrounds, and to chase laughter rising from a baby's lips like bubbles on the wind rather than to chase dust bunnies beneath beds! Amen.

*Happy is he with such a mother!
Faith in womankind beats with his
blood and trust in all things high
comes easy to him.*

—Alfred, Lord Tennyson

April 24

My soul finds rest in God.

Psalm 62:1 NIV

Lord, I believe a rest remains,
   To all Thy people known;
A rest where pure enjoyment reigns
And thou art loved alone;
A rest where all our soul's desire
Is fixed on things above;
where fear and sin and grief expire,
Cast out by perfect love.

—Charles Wesley

*When I pray, I like to picture myself, small and insignificant,
huddling in the comforting shadow of Almighty God
as though He were an actual fortress, a high tower
directly above me. It's easier to pray when I feel
that protected, that sheltered.*

—Joni Eareckson Tada, *Seeking God*

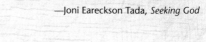

April 25

Let the little children come to me, and do not stop them;
for it is to such as these that the kingdom of heaven belongs.

Matthew 19:14

ord God, please give me an answer to this dilemma. I want my small children to be in church, to absorb the sounds and scenes of worship, and to feel at home there. But it is so difficult to keep them all quiet at the same time. By the time one child is settled, another is wiggly and ready to cause a disturbance. My anger and embarrassment flare, and I can't even concentrate on the sermon. At the end of the service, I've done anything but worship, and I am so frustrated I want to cry.

Examine my motives, Lord. You welcomed children to your kingdom. Am I wrong to want my children in church with me? Please help me to come up with solutions and make the right decisions.

Goals are better reached in small steps than in one giant leap.

April 26

O Lord, our Sovereign, how majestic is your name in all the earth!
You have set your glory above the heavens. . . . When I look at your
heavens, the work of your fingers, the moon and the stars that you have
established; what are human beings that you are mindful of them?

Psalm 8:1,3–4

A s I follow in the children's wake as they
discover bugs, plants, and cloud faces, your
awesome creations bring us
to our knees in daily thankfulness as we learn to name
and know the works of
your hands,
Loving Creator.

God writes the Gospel
not in the Bible alone,
but on trees, and flowers,
and clouds and stars.

—Martin Luther

April 27

Until now you have not asked for anything in my name.
Ask and you will receive, so that your joy may be complete.

John 16:24

Lord Jesus, you are medicine to me when I am
sick, strength to me when I need help, life itself
when I fear death, the way when I long for heaven, the
light when all is dark, and food when I need nourishment. Glory be to you forever. Amen.

—St. Ambrose

Let God take care of your problems;
cast your care upon Him and do what He
has instructed you to do. It almost sounds
too good to be true, doesn't it?
You can actually enjoy life
while God handles all your problems!

—Joyce Meyer

April 28

I have come to do your will, O God.

Hebrews 10:7

If I am right, thy grace impart,
    Still in the right to stay;
If I am wrong, O teach my heart
To find that better way.

Save me alike from foolish Pride
Or impious Discontent,
At aught thy wisdom has denied,
Or aught thy goodness lent.

Teach me to feel another's woe,
To hide the fault I see:
That mercy I to others show,
That mercy show to me.

Mean tho' I am, not wholly so,
Since quicken'd by thy breath;
O lead me, wheresoe'er I go
Thro' this day's life or death!

This day be bread and peace my lot:
All else beneath the sun
Thou know'st if best bestow'd or not,
And let thy will be done.

—Alexander Pope, "Universal Prayer"

April 29

So I will seek out my sheep.

Ezekiel 34:12

On days when laundry, appointments, phone calls, and other interruptions bury me, I know that, as eagerly as a child spots characters in hidden object picture books, the God of lost sheep finds me, and I am restored.

Make this home worthy of the presence of Jesus the Unseen Guest. Let him be your guide in speech and conduct. Dedicate each day's activities to the glory of God.

—James L. Christensen,
New Ways to Worship

April 30

He makes his sun rise on the evil and on the good, and sends rain on the righteous and on the unrighteous.

Matthew 5:45

Father, rainy days can be so difficult with a house full of restless children. Several days of rain in a row can be nearly impossible. It is a challenge to keep everyone occupied with worthwhile activities.

Lord, you send the sun and rain in equal measure. How can I be thankful for one and not the other? Help me see the beauty in both. I ask for your gifts of grace and peace and an extra dose of resourcefulness to help me survive.

You can't appreciate the sunny days unless you've experienced the rain.

My Prayer Life

_____

_____

_____

_____

_____

_____

_____

_____

_____

_____

_____

God, make me brave for life,
Oh, braver than this!
Let me straighten after pain
As a tree straightens after the rain.
Shining and lovely again.

God make me brave for life,
Much braver than this!
As the blown grass lifts let me rise
From sorrow with quiet eyes
Knowing Thy way is wise.

God make me brave—Life brings
Such blinding things,
Help me to keep my sight,
Help me to see aright
That out of the dark—comes light.

—Grace Noll Crowell, *Songs for Courage*

God will never disappoint us. He loves us and has only one purpose for us: holiness, which in his kingdom equals joy.

—Elisabeth Elliot, *Discipline—The Glad Surrender*

O God, from my youth you have taught me, and I still proclaim your wondrous deeds. So even to old age and gray hairs, O God, do not forsake me, until I proclaim your might to all the generations to come.

Psalm 71:17–18

thank you, God, that I'm not the same person today as I was even just a few years ago. This new life as a mother writes its changing tale on my heart, face, and mind like growth rings on a tree. May this tree of life continue to grow into the future where I will provide limbs of love from which my children can launch their own lives.

When the Lord touches our lives, our character becomes more like Christ's.

May 3

The Lord is near to all who call on him, to all who call on him in truth.

Psalm 145:18

Lord, at this time when our country observes a national day of prayer, I thank you for your faithfulness. Your promise to be near me and to hear my prayers gives me courage, comfort, and hope.

As a mother, I need your continual guidance. No matter how hopeless a situation may seem, you have the answers. As I pray, I feel your  peace filling up the empty places of my flagging spirit and bringing sweet relief. I feel your wisdom pointing my thoughts toward new ideas and solutions.

Forgive me for the times I have prayed selfishly or have not prayed at all. Let me not forget to pray for others as well as my family and to pray believing that you will answer.

May 4

Dear Lord,

Give me strength when the children scream just a decibel too loud.

Give me patience when they spill their food and break my favorite vase.

Give me hope when it seems they will never obey my slightest wish.

Give me humor when my littlest ones decide they can't make it to the bathroom.

Give me rest when the long day threatens to spill over into night.

Give me gratitude when I watch them sleep at night, knowing I'll have to do it all over again tomorrow.

Amen.

May 5

They shall be like a tree planted by water, sending out its roots by the stream. It shall not fear when heat comes, and its leaves shall stay green; in the year of drought it is not anxious, and it does not cease to bear fruit.

Jeremiah 17:8

Mothering is such a promising vocation. She is like a gardener who tends her garden with care.

Sometimes it is amazing how much you can learn from your children.

—Ray Pritchard, *The ABC's of Wisdom*

May 6

A friend loves at all times.

Proverbs 17:17

Now, into the keeping of God I put
All doings of today
All disappointments,
hindrances,
forgotten things,
negligence.
All gladness and beauty,
love,
delight,
achievement.
All that people have done for me,
All that I have done for them,
my work and my prayers.
And I commit all the people whom I love
to his shepherding,
to his healing and restoring,
to his calling and making
Through Jesus Christ our Lord.

—Margaret Cropper

May 7

y Lord Jesus, You have blessed me way beyond my ability to thank You. If this were a contest between Your blessing and my thankfulness, You would win hands down. Still, I'd like to compete by showering You with thankfulness every day. Open my eyes to all the ways You're blessing me, and I will give You thanks. Amen.

—Barbara Johnson, *Boomerang Joy*

Count your blessings, name them one by one:
Count your blessings, see what God hath done.
Count your blessings, name them one by one;
Count your many blessings, see what God hath done.

—Johnson Oatman Jr., "Count Your Blessings"

May 8

Lord, teach us to pray.

Luke 11:1

Dear Jesus, how desperately I need to learn to pray. And yet when I am honest, I know that I often do not even want to pray.

I am distracted!

I am stubborn!

I am self-centered!

In your mercy, Jesus, bring my "want-er" more in line with your "need-er" so that I can come to want what I need.

In your name and for our sake, I pray. Amen.

—Richard J. Foster, *Prayer—Finding the Heart's True Home*

May 9

We who are strong ought to put up with the failings of the weak, and not to please ourselves. . . . For Christ did not please himself; but, as it is written, "The insults of those who insult you have fallen on me."

Romans 15:1, 3

Father, one of the difficult things about being a mother is to teach my children to be tolerant of others who are not like them. In spite of my efforts, my children are capable of following the crowd—ridiculing, jeering, or being insensitive to the feelings and needs of others.

You have always taught us by example, showing us how to love the stranger, to withhold judgment, to help the ungodly, and to bear the weaknesses of others. Your son kept company with outcasts and took on their burdens.

Stir up in us and our children, Lord, your compassion for the person who is different, and help us to understand this truth: We *are* our brother's keepers.

May 10

Dear God,

The long and loud and noisy day threatens to overwhelm me, and there are still so many hours to go
before I sleep. Will it ever end?   Will I ever know
the precious sound of golden
silence? God, give me the gift of
inner peace so that no matter
how loud the baby cries or
how many times the phone
rings or how grating the sound
of my boss's voice gets in my
ear, I will be able to crawl safe
and secure into my inner sanc-
tuary and find the renewal
I need to do it all again
tomorrow.

Amen!

*My mother had a great deal of trouble
with me, but I think she enjoyed it.*

—Mark Twain

May 11

The Lord will guide you continually, and satisfy your needs.

Isaiah 58:11

Guide me, O God, to savor today and all that is yet to be discovered at the hands of my children. I know that what came before and what is yet to be form a marvelous mosaic of the whole.

May 12

I feel your hand on mine as I learn to be a good mother, O God, knowing that together you and I are instilling lifelong values and beliefs in my children. I wish it were a straight-lined experience, but for me, it is more like a zigzag, making my growth seem slow. And yet, I am grateful for all the help you give me.

Like toddlers we take a few small steps forward each day and try to relish the moments. By focusing on one day at a time, eventually we can look back and we are amazed at how far we've come on this bumpy road.

—Jan Markell,
Waiting for a Miracle

May 13

Honor your father and your mother.

Exodus 20:12

Caring God, it took becoming a mother myself to understand the depth of my mother's love for me. Only now can I comprehend how much she sacrificed day by day for my happiness and well-being.

Your love and sacrifice were her model, and now I, too, understand, through my mother, the extent of your love for me. So on this day to honor mothers, I also honor and praise you, Lord. You taught us how to love, and everything we both learned about being a mother, we learned from you.

A mother's love is the closest thing we know to God's love.

May 14

As a mother comforts her child, so I will comfort you; you shall be comforted in Jerusalem. You shall see, and your heart shall rejoice; your bodies shall flourish like the grass.

Isaiah 66:13–14

Mother and Father of Creation,
We give thanks to you for our mothers.
We thank you, and them,
For the nurture, love and providence
Which they have bestowed upon us.
Bless them in their work,
Bless them in their leisure,
Bless them in the depth of their hearts.
Fill their days with wonder,
Their nights with peaceful rest,
And their lives with the presence
Of your eternal love
Amen.

—Vienna Cobb Anderson

*Motherhood is a sacrifice. That is why
the mother becomes the symbol of Mother Earth.
She is the one who has given birth to us and
on whom we live and on whose body we find food.*

—Joseph Campbell

May 15

Let me but live my life from year to year,
　　With forward face and unreluctant soul;
Not hurrying to, nor turning from, the goal;
Not mourning for the things that disappear
In the dim past, nor holding back in fear
From what the future veils; but with a whole
And happy heart, that pays its toll
To Youth and Age, and travels on with cheer.

—Henry Van Dyke

*I have felt assured that I do not have to fear the future
because God is already there.*

—Fran Caffey Sandin, *See You Later, Jeffrey*

May 16

Her children arise and call her blessed.

Proverbs 31:28 NIV

I am woman, giver of life.
I am mother, wife, friend,
and family member.
I am neighbor and concerned citizen.
I am pregnant with possibilities for the future
and remembrances of the past.
I give birth to children and to new ideas.
I nurture everyone around me
and empower them to be their best.
I am a lover, an adventurer, a guardian angel.
I am woman, giver of life.

*Life—personal life, meaningful life, human life in its deepest,
lasting sense—exists in the womb from conception.*

—Jack Hayford, *I'll Hold You in Heaven*

May 17

God, give me strength. Please give me strength!
When my little girl breaks my favorite crystal bud vase,
And my son gets permanent marker on his hands and face,
And I find old candy wrappers all over the place,
God, give me strength!

God, give me strength. Please give me strength!
When my daughter's sleepovers get way out of hand,
And I find her bad report card tucked behind her bedstand,
When my older son says college isn't part of his plan,
And instead decides he'd rather join the local punk band,
God, give me strength. Please give me strength!

May 18

A cheerful heart is a good medicine,
but a downcast spirit dries up the bones.

Proverbs 17:22

Dear Lord, life can easily become too serious when motherly responsibilities overwhelm me. As I deal with my children each day, let me not forget my sense of humor. Humor can soothe ruffled feelings, calm tempers, and lighten our moods when we become too somber.

Laughter can diffuse tension, chase away anger, and make forgiveness easier. It's even good for our health.

Lord, I thank you for your healing gift of humor. Grant to my children, also, the ability to enjoy the humorous side of life and receive all of its benefits.

Humor is the oil that keeps
the machinery of life humming.

May 19

I appeal to you therefore, brothers and sisters, by the mercies of God, to present your bodies as a living sacrifice, holy and acceptable to God, which is your spiritual worship.

Romans 12:1

Almighty God, my Father and my Savior: I
offer thee my whole self for thy use this day.
I offer thee my work; my thought and reading; my
contacts with people; my rest and my recreation; my
joys and my sorrows; my sufferings and my tempta-
tions. Do thy will in me all day long.
Direct, control, suggest this day,
All I design, or do, or say,
That all my powers, with all their might,
In thy sole glory may unite.

—Olive Wyon, *Prayer*

In the infinite resignation there is peace and rest.

—Søren Kierkegaard

May 20

God give me joy in the common things;
    In the dawn that lures, the eve that sings.
In the new grass sparkling after rain,
In the late wind's wild and weird refrain;
In the springtime's spacious field of gold,
In the precious light by winter doled.
God give me joy in the love of friends,
In their dear home talk as summer ends;
In the songs of children, unrestrained;
In the sober wisdom age has gained.
God give me joy in the tasks that press,
In the memories that burn and bless;
In the thought that life has love to spend,
In the faith that God's at journey's end.
God give me hope for each day that springs,
God give me joy in the common things!

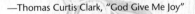

—Thomas Curtis Clark, "God Give Me Joy"

May 21

This is the day that the Lord has made; let us rejoice and be glad in it.

Psalm 118:24

*L*ord, may I be wakeful at sunrise to begin a new day for you, cheerful at sunset for having done my work for you; thankful at moonrise and under starshine for the beauty of the universe. And may I add what little may be in me to your great world.

—The Abbot of Greve

Even before opening your eyes, listen to that inner voice inviting you to yet another glorious adventure at the hands of a child. God is holding both of you.

May 22

Loving God, sometimes when my children and I have a difference of opinion, they translate that difference as a lack of care for them. Everything I do is for them. How can I convince them that I am on their side—that my opposition to their opinions or actions grows out of my love and concern for them?

I want my children to know that my love, my help, my forgiveness, are there for the taking; that I am always ready to listen to and comfort them.

Lord, your great love has at times been misunderstood and misinterpreted by your children. You have been down this same road. Help me to demonstrate that I care. Let my love penetrate the walls that go up between me and my children, just as your love has done when I've turned away from you.

Love sometimes forces us to take opposite sides.

May 23

May the Lord give strength to his people!

Psalm 29:11

*L*ord, may I be secure enough in You
    That I can stand up under any painful dart
That tells me I'm not being received
With a standing ovation.

—Jan Markell, *Waiting for a Miracle*

Greatness lies not in being strong,
but in the right use of strength.

—Henry Ward Beecher

May 24

God is exalted in his power; who is a teacher like him?

Job 36:22

Father, as the school year winds down, I pray for my children's teachers. I thank you for the good ones—for their talent, their sensitivity, and their dedication. In the coming months, grant these good men and women a time of restoration, so they may return to their jobs refreshed, with a new attitude and a godly perspective.

For those teachers who have not lived up to expectations, I ask your special care. Supply their needs, Lord, and stir up in them the will and desire to do their best.

Please find us more teachers who are right for our children; those who are willing to follow your lead. I know that all good teaching comes from you, Lord. You are the Master Teacher.

Teachers are your partners in your child's education.

May 25

*You have been born anew, not of perishable but of imperishable seed,
through the living and enduring word of God.*

1 Peter 1:23

ternal Spirit, we turn from the noise and hurrying of life to the peace that can be found only in thy presence. Forgive us for falling under the domination of material things, for becoming dull and selfish. Forgive us for the restlessness that afflicts us, for lack of self-possession and serenity of spirit. Enter into our minds, we pray thee. Free us from serfdom to things and from confusion of thought. O thou who transforms the hearts of those who seek thee, teach us to cultivate the quiet mind, which knows how to turn to thee in time of turmoil and be at peace.

—Robert Merrill Bartlett

May 26

Beloved, let us love one another, because love is from God;
everyone who loves is born of God and knows God.

1 John 4:7

Heavenly Father, every time I feel sad or lonely, my mind flashes back to thoughts of my mother, gathering me in her arms, stroking my hair, and crooning sweet songs to soothe away hurts. She cared for me so tenderly, I want to cry for the beauty of those times. She loved me, Lord, because she loved you first.

Soon she will no longer be able to do things for herself. How long will it be, I wonder, before we completely exchange roles—when I will be the mother and she will become the child.

The time is coming, Lord. I pray that with your help, I can be for her what she has always been for me: your wondrous love personified.

I am becoming my mother's mother.

May 27

My help comes from the Lord, who made heaven and earth.

Psalm 121:2

You give your help, O Comforting God, not in proportion to our merit, but based only on our need. For you come not only to those who are "keeping it together," but to those of us who are fragmented and fractured. I need the tenderness of your caress so that I know I am not alone in my awful feelings of weakness.

The armor of God will shield us from dangers we haven't even thought of yet.

May 28

The Lord will guide you continually . . . and you shall be like a watered garden, like a spring of water, whose waters never fail.

Holy Spirit, empower me with the vitality to keep up with these kids.

Embolden me with courage to face each day's pressing problems.

Enlighten me with creative ways to juggle the responsibilities in front of me.

Enrich my inner world so that when my outer world goes crazy, I don't go crazy along with it!

Embrace me when I am too tired, too scared, and too insecure to make even the smallest decision.

Entertain me when they've all gone off to work and school and I am home alone again.

Thank you, Holy Spirit.

You must watch how much you give, and serve your own needs while you continue to serve your children. It's paradoxical, but if you give them too much of yourself, you are not really doing them the service that you think you are as a parent and a guiding force.

—Sanford J. Matthews, M.D., and Maryann Bucknum Brinley

May 29

Pay to all what is due them—taxes to whom taxes are due,
revenue to whom revenue is due, respect to whom respect is due,
honor to whom honor is due.

Romans 13:7

Lord, you have told us to "remember the days of old." Memorials have played a large part in the history of your people in Israel, and we thank you for these reminders to honor the past.

As we remember those who have gone before us, we teach our children love and respect for life itself.

In giving honor to others, we thank and honor you, O God, for your love and for the great sacrifice of your son, Jesus Christ.

To honor our past is to enrich our future.

May 30

O Lord, our Sovereign, how majestic is your name in all the earth!

Psalm 8:9

Like a stream, the whole world pours into our
   lives, our eyes, our hands, and fills our souls
with living gladness.
O Lord, our God
How excellent is Thy name.

Amen!

—James L. Christensen, *New Ways to Worship*

*Today dawned like any other
and then "it" happened—
completely unexpectedly.
I saw in you, through you,
with you a glimpse of heaven.*

—Robin Jones Gunn, *Mothering by Heart*

May 31

Be strong and courageous; do not be frightened or dismayed, for the Lord your God is with you wherever you go.

Joshua 1:9

Lord, a child's fears and anxieties are a real concern to a mother. We can usually calm younger children's fears, but, as they grow older, youngsters are exposed to horrible sights and sounds on TV, which can raise terror in the bravest of us. I can't always control situations that cause my children to be afraid, but you can. You can conquer the mightiest enemy. Lift us up, Lord. Help us to put to rest some of those fears and to build in our children a quiet confidence that you will protect them. Give them a sense of your presence, and let them know you are with them wherever they go.

My Prayer Life

_____

_____

_____

_____

_____

_____

_____

_____

_____

June 1

Give me neither poverty nor riches; feed me with the food that I need.

Proverbs 30:8

Lord, as I struggle to balance my budget, I ask myself: What is wealth? Is it having material riches, plenty of food, clothing, a house, and freedom from worry about money?

You have taught me, Father, that it is none of these things. True wealth is having work to do. It is being cared for by a loving God. It is enjoying the love of friends and family. It is being a mother.

You give me all I need or want, Lord. I am the wealthiest of women.

Wealth is not measured in money and possessions;
it is a state of mind.

June 2

He has made everything beautiful in its time.

Ecclesiastes 3:11 NIV

God of all creation, I thank you for the beauty of the earth. Every leaf, every grain of sand, sings of your love. Each creature reveals your unique artistry. The sun and stars bear witness to your greatness.

You have woven together a natural world full of surprises for us to enjoy and mysteries for us to solve, and you have made us the stewards of this vast treasury. Thank you for your confidence in us.

In your unfailing goodness, I pray that you will pass on to my children and my children's children the love for this sacred earth. Help them care for it, preserve it, and forever wonder at its grandeur.

June 3

The human mind plans the way, but the Lord directs the steps.

Proverbs 16:9

Take my hand, Lord, and lead me through this day, step by step. Remind me that I cannot do everything I wish, nor do any of it perfectly. Only you are perfect, and only with your help can I do my best. Help me to remember to ask you for help.

—Avery Brooke, Plain Prayers for a Complicated World

Do not rule out God's help with the small details of life.
After all, details make up the totality of life.
If we do not let God into our everyday lives,
he may not be able to intervene in the crises.

—Catherine Marshall, Beyond Ourselves

June 4

Do not provoke your children.

Colossians 3:21

n your wisdom, you designed us to reject the word "don't." Like all your children, mine do better with "do" words. *Do* love, share, work, tend, tolerate, obey, forgive. Help me say "do" as often as I can. Let me be a positive example of your vision.

Peace is not the absence of conflict, but the handling of conflict without loss of balance.

—Rabbi Rami M. Shapiro

June 5

Rejoice always, pray continually, give thanks in all circumstances; for this is God's will for you in Christ Jesus.

1 Thessalonians 5:16–18 NIV

I have prayed about this burden, this emergency, and now, Lord, I will deliberately fix my heart on praising you even before I see the answer. The answer to my prayer hasn't come yet, but I expect it. And my praise—a sacrifice—is my offering to you in demonstration of my belief and confidence.

—Joni Eareackson Tada,
Glorious Intruder

Everything is safe which we commit to Him, and nothing is really safe which is not so committed.

—A. W. Tozer, *The Pursuit of God*

June 6

If you want to learn, then go and ask the wild animals and the birds, the flowers and the fish. Any of them can tell you what the Lord has done. Every living creature is in the hands of God.

Job 12:7–10 CEV

Lord, with the ending of the school year, the children have the luxury of endless unscheduled days stretched out before them. Father, please help them be resourceful in filling their days with pleasurable and worthwhile activities. Keep them safe from the dangers of the season, and help them to enjoy the freedom of the outdoors.

Summer is a time for unique experiences. As you keep my children in your care, Lord, afford them the opportunity for many different kinds of learning not possible in a classroom. May many outdoor experiences increase my children's awe and wonder over all that you have given them.

Summer break is an education all its own.

June 7

All your children shall be taught by the Lord,
and great shall be the prosperity of your children.

Isaiah 54:13

Father, I feel relief that this school year, with all of its ups and downs, is at a close. Yet I can't help wondering how the children will fare next year. Will the work be too hard or too easy? Will they be able to hold their own? Will new teachers be sensitive to their needs? Will unexpected occurrences suddenly change everything? So many questions, and so much anxiety.

Lord, please put my worries to rest. May I learn to rely on you and take one step at a time through this maze called motherhood. I am reassured by your Word that all of my children are in your hands. Please prepare the hearts and minds of the teachers, and let them be used by you. Amen.

June 8

O give thanks unto the Lord, for he is good,
for his steadfast love endures forever.

Psalm 136:1

Joyful, joyful, we adore thee,
God of glory, Lord of love;
Hearts unfold like flowers before thee,
Opening to the sun above.
Melt the clouds of sin and sadness;
Drive the dark of doubt away;
Giver of immortal gladness,
Fill us with the light of day!

Thou art giving and forgiving,
Ever blessing, ever blest,
Well-spring of the joy of living,
Ocean-depth of happy rest!
Thou our Father, Christ our Brother,—
All who live in love are thine:
Teach us how to love each other,
Lift us to the Joy Divine.

—Henry Van Dyke, "Hymn of Joy"

June 9

The wind blows where it chooses, and you hear the sound of it,
but you do not know where it comes from or where it goes.
So it is with everyone who is born of the Spirit.

John 3:8

When the winds of change and challenge blow hard into my life, I will take refuge in you, O Lord. When the darkness descends upon my house and home, I will fear not for I will place my faith in you, O Lord. When my child is ill or my husband is hurt, I will remain steadfast, for I know that you will be right there by my side, O Lord. Although I cannot see you, I know you are always with me, O Lord, and in that I take comfort and find strength.

There is no great and no small
To the soul that maketh all;
And where it cometh, all things are;
And it cometh everywhere.

—Ralph Waldo Emerson

June 10

It is good to give thanks to the Lord,
to sing praises to your name, O Most High.

Psalm 92:1

Lord, each day you furnish us with our daily bread. You feed and nourish us, yet often we neglect to acknowledge your gifts of food.

Forgive us, Father, for our selfishness and our disregard for your faithful care. We know that prayer should be a necessary part of every meal.

If, in our haste, we forget to thank you, Lord, remind us of our rudeness. Our meals are not complete until we thank the Giver for his many gifts.

Prayer before meals improves the appetite.

June 11

The Lord, your God, is in your midst, a warrior who gives victory;
he will rejoice over you with gladness, he will renew you in his love;
he will exult over you with loud singing.

Zephaniah 3:17

Gently, Lord
    Love me gently.
I'm hurting now.
I've lived to see your sovereignty.
You've taught my knees to bow.
I've caught glimpses of your glory.
I've seen your righteous ways.
But right now I need you, Father,
Just to face another day.

You have promised not to always be
Exactly what I please
But You give me sweet assurance
You're exactly what I need.
I need a gentle Father
And the lullaby He sings,
"Let Me tuck you safely
Underneath My healing wings."

—Beth Moore, *Things Pondered*

June 12

You are a God ready to forgive, gracious and merciful,
slow to anger and abounding in steadfast love.

Nehemiah 9:17

ather, help me not to take myself so seriously;
Not to strive for perfection...
help me to be content to be worthy in Your eyes alone.

—Jan Markell, *Waiting for a Miracle*

When it seems that scarcely a day ends by saying,
"If only I could do it over. I regret what I said, did,
or didn't do," the God of fresh starts is eager to
make things right. All you need to say is, "Forgive me for
today, and redeem me for tomorrow."

June 13

Let all who take refuge in you rejoice; let them ever sing for joy.

Psalm 5:11

God bless this joyful life I have been given, this honor of being called "mother," "wife," and "caretaker." God bless my husband, my children, and my home. God bless my friends and neighbors and the people I meet along the way. God bless the joy and the pain, the pleasure and the frustration. God bless every moment of it, every load of laundry, every carpool day, every late night stolen moment with my spouse, every phone call that interrupts dinner, every skinned knee and broken heart. God bless it all!

Alas! By some degree of woe
We every bliss must gain;
The heart can ne'er a transport know
That never feels a pain.

—Lord Lyttleton

June 14

O God, hear us as...
    We pray for mothers
who bake bread from scratch and
who help find lost keys, mittens, and school books.
We pray for those
who steal bread crusts for supper,
who need no keys: Cardboard houses don't lock.
We pray for those
who balance career, family, and self with energy
    left over.
We pray for mothers
who work two and three jobs and have nothing
    left over.
We pray for our mothers
who dreamed we'd succeed at whatever we wanted
as we now yearn for our offspring's success.
And we pray for mothers
who dream for their offspring but can only
measure success by keeping them alive.
Amen.

June 15

Ye have wept in the ears of the Lord.

"It's not fair!" is a phrase mothers hear regularly, Lord. Are we really being unfair in our dealings with our children, or are they merely complaining?

Just as the Israelites complained to you while being fed in the wilderness, so today's children feel cheated because a gift is the "wrong" shape, brand, or color.

Lord of peace, wrap us in your love, and dispel the cloud of discontent that hangs over our children. Guard us from weeping in your ear. Take away our complaining spirits, and sprinkle us with the gentle rain of forgiveness.

Complaining is just another name for ingratitude.

June 16

Lord, what I am going through right now isn't the end of my story. Every tomorrow is still in Your hand. My next moment, the very next breath I draw, is a gift from You. I offer You my burdens and say, "Whatever, Lord." I rest now, relieved that You have joy ahead for me. Full, overflowing joy. Amen.

—Barbara Johnson, *Boomerang Joy*

God hath not promised
Skies ever blue,
Flower strewn pathways
All our lives through;
God hath not promised
Sun without rain,
Joy without sorrow,
Peace without pain.
But God hath promised
Strength for the day,
Rest for the labor,
Light for the way,
Grace for the trials,
Help from above,
Unfailing sympathy,
Undying love.

—Annie Johnson Flint

June 17

Love does not demand its own way.

1 Corinthians 13:5 LB

Dear God, sometimes I get angry so easily. Things go wrong, people don't act the way I want them to, someone's words rub me the wrong way. Help me, Father, to control my anger, to keep it from spilling out, hurting those around me. Remind me that usually, when it comes right down to it, I'm angry simply because I can't have my own way. Give me the strength to accept whatever you send into my life.

—*Light for My Path*

June 18

A faithful man who can find?

Proverbs 20:6 KJV

My heart is full of gratitude, O God, when I think of my husband and the miraculous way you brought us together. I realize now it was you who chose him to be the father of my children.

He is a man of integrity and worth, generous and loving, with the ability to laugh at himself: a perfect combination for a parent.

His loyalty and faithfulness are unquestioned. I am proud to be his wife and prouder still to have my children call him Dad. I humbly thank you, Lord, for this uncommon blessing you have given to me and our children: a faithful man and a man of faith.

Show me a father who loves his child unconditionally, and I'll show you a child who is comfortable with the world.

June 19

Open my eyes, so that I may behold wondrous things.

Psalm 119:18

Bless to me, O God, the earth
    beneath my feet,
Bless to me, O God, the path whereon I go,
Bless to me, O God, the people whom I meet,
Today, tonight and tomorrow.

—Celtic Blessing

*Lie on your back in the freshly cut grass
and count stars in the midnight navy blue sky—
and know there is much of life yet
to discover and enjoy.*

June 20

O Lord our God,
   You are the great God.
You are the creator of life;
You make the regions above
and sustain the earth from which we live.
You are the hunter who hunts for souls.
You are the leader who goes before us.
You are the great mantle which covers us.
You are the one whose hands are with wounds.
You are the one whose blood is a living stream.
Today we say thank you, our God
and come before you in silent praise.

—Kathy Keay

*Backyard adventures, like discovering the migrating butterflies
that stopped to rest in the trees, draw us into accepting our
role as caretakers of God's marvelous creation,
a daily reminder of God's presence in our lives.*

June 21

Lord, how reassuring it is for me and my children to know something in the world is constant. You send the seasons in your perfect timing, and summer has arrived on schedule. I thank you for this season of warmth and relaxation. It is good to see my children enjoy freedom from the cares and pressures of the school year.

Please guard and protect them through these months, and use this time to restore their energy and enthusiasm to meet the demands of the coming school year.

Surround us all with the beauty of earth's summer wardrobe, and accept our gratitude for the friendliest season of all.

Summer is the carefree season.

Whoever walks with the wise becomes wise,
but the companion of fools suffers harm.

Proverbs 13:20

Heavenly Father, as my children grow older, their choice of companions becomes crucial. Today I pray for my children's friends, for the safety and welfare of my children are tied up in theirs.

I pray for good companions for each child: friends who will be loyal, who won't lead them into trouble, and whose traits will complement those of my children. May my youngsters be good friends in return.

Lord, you keep track of each of your sheep. Please keep your loving eyes on these, and draw them continually back into your fold.

A good friend is a gift God has chosen just for you.

June 23

For those who enter God's rest also cease from their labors as God did from his.

Hebrews 4:10

hat a wonderful day! And now, God of rest and peace, the children are sleeping, replete with the joys of our summer discoveries that they are savoring to the last drop. We celebrate the joy of ordinary days and rest in your care.

Every day I meet God in my kitchen among the pots and pans, the meat and mashed potatoes.

June 24

Lord, I'm often tempted to go inside myself. I think I can make my spiritual life a do-it-yourself project. But you have said in your Word that two are better than one, that Jesus is present where two or three are gathered in his name. May my life with you find a dwelling amid a community of friends. Help me to find partners and mentors who can encourage my faith, and to whom I can give as well. Lead me to those with whom I can join arms and find new strength to move forward. Amen.

—Timothy Jones, *The Art of Prayer*

Child, even this day, trust! And to-morrow have faith,
And on all to-morrows! The darkness grows less.
Trust! And each day when first gleams the dawn-breath,
Awake thou to pray; God is wakeful to bless!

—Victor Hugo, "Trust in God"

Oh, I have fared through laughter 'neath skies of
    summer blue!
And many an hour of mirth and joy I've danced and
    scampered through,
But, Lord, when joy was mine to know, I gave no
    thought to you.
I've whistled down the summer wind, I've sung a merry
    tune.
We never think of winter's snow when we are deep in
    June,
And no one dreams when pleasure calls that it will go
    so soon.
But, Lord, the skies are gray to-day and I am deep in care,
And I have need for help and strength my weight of
    grief to bear,
And so, like many an erring son, I turn to thee in prayer.

—Edgar Guest, "In Time Of Trial"

There are still mothers who will ever hold
The old sweet ways of truth and righteousness
Before their children's eyes, who long have told
Christ's teachings to their young to heal and bless.
Thank God for any mother, anywhere,
Who loves and serves, and finds her strength in prayer.

—Grace Noll Crowell, "There Are Still Mothers," *Songs of Faith*

June 26

And let the peace of Christ rule in your hearts.

Colossians 3:15

Lord, make me an instrument of your peace.
Where there is hatred, let me sow love;
Where there is injury, pardon;
Where there is doubt, faith;
Where there is despair, hope;
Where there is darkness, light;
And where there is sadness, joy.
O, Divine Master, grant that I may
not so much seek to be
consoled, as to console;
To be understood as to
understand;
To be loved as to love;
For it is in giving that we receive;
It is in pardoning that we are pardoned;
It is in dying that we are born to eternal life.

—St. Francis of Assisi

June 27

The purposes in the human mind are like deep water,
but the intelligent will draw them out.

Proverbs 20:5

ord, I do have this life! I do want to live it to the
full. Don't let me miss anything good, or scorn
those who find what I have missed.

—James L. Christensen, *New Ways to Worship*

Being optimistic and
upbuilding with the children
is a daily choice that
is decided with
both the mind
and the heart.

June 28

Come, you that are blessed by my Father,
inherit the kingdom prepared for you.

Matthew 25:34

I wonder who I will be today. Will I be the woman, the individual spirit with individual hopes and dreams? Will I be the loving and supportive wife? Maybe I'll be called upon to be the good friend, the one who listens and offers sage advice. Will I be the perfect employee, who gets the job done right and on time? I imagine I will also have to be the mother, who cleans up after and prods along and scolds and loves and forgives. Then again, it will probably be a day just like any other, when I will be called upon to be all these things and more. Lord, no matter what this day brings, help me get through it with your loving guidance. Amen.

The many different roles a woman plays in life are all part of the wholeness and perfection of who she truly is.

June 29

The Lord will watch over your coming and going both now and forevermore.

Psalm 121:8 NIV

Lord, our vacation time is coming, and with it will be long stretches of travel with the kids. Help us to plan adequately so the trip will go smoothly. Guard us from petty bickering and turn this trip into an opportunity for happy anticipation, recreation, and learning.

May this time of togetherness bond us more deeply as a family and draw us closer to you, O Lord.

Most of all, surround us with your presence so we may rest in safety on your loving shoulders. Amen.

Take God along on your vacation.
He is your strongest seatbelt
and your greatest safety net.

June 30

God opposes the proud, but gives grace to the humble.

1 Peter 5:5

Gracious God, being a mother is the most important calling of my life, but I confess that it has been difficult to keep going at such an exhausting pace. Pride has kept me from asking for help, but where is it written that I alone must fulfill all of my children's needs?

Lord, break down this barrier of pride within me, and make me humble enough to admit to others that I need help. My husband, parents, and friends are capable of sharing the load, if only I will let them.

Help me to convince myself that I need a break once in a while, that I am not being selfish when I take one, and that a relaxed mother can be a more loving mother.

There are two kinds of pride:
One is self-respect; the other is conceit—
an exaggerated view of your own abilities.

My Prayer Life

_____

_____

_____

_____

_____

_____

_____

_____

_____

_____

July 1

Great is thy faithfulness, O God my Father,
There is no shadow of turning with thee;
Thou changest not, thy compassions they fail not;
As thou hast been thou forever wilt be.

Pardon for sin and a peace that
endureth,
Thine own dear presence to cheer
and to guide;
Strength for today and bright hope for
tomorrow,
Blessings all mine, with ten thousand
beside!

Great is thy faithfulness! Great is thy
faithfulness!
Morning by morning new mercies I see;
All I have needed thy hand hath provided.
Great is thy faithfulness, Lord unto me.

—Thomas O. Chisholm

*Hang on to this. God still loves you. He loves you
as much in the darkness as He does in the light.*

—Ray Pritchard, *The Road Best Traveled*

July 2

I prayed for this child, and the Lord has granted me what I asked of him.

1 Samuel 1:27 NIV

Dear God, I thank you for the gift of this child to raise, this life to share, this mind to help mold, this body to nurture, and this spirit to enrich.

Let me never betray this child's trust, dampen this child's hope, or discourage this child's dreams.

Help me dear God to help this precious child become all you mean him to be.

Let your grace and love fall on him like gentle breezes and give him inner strength and peace and patience for the journey ahead.

—Marian Wright Edelman, *Guide My Feet*

I know God is already with this child ... and with me, too.
For in the conception and gestation,
I'm also growing a new me, a mother.
A blessed creation.

July 3

Therefore, my beloved, be steadfast, immovable, always excelling in the work of the Lord, because you know that in the Lord your labor is not in vain.

1 Corinthians 15:58

What lasts when raising children? We bring this to you, O God, and get the answer: Relationships of love. Love, steadfast and loyal despite tantrums. Love, patient and humorous. Love, offered without strings. Love, invested without requiring a guaranteed return. Love, as I feel it from you, landing dove-soft on my outstretched hands, folding into hugs around me and my children. Thank you for teaching us how to love.

Our God is a persistent God. Because He is eternal, He knows no finality. He never quits. Knowing that should give us enough faith and hope to keep us doing our part as Christian parents.

—Margie M. Lewis, *The Hurting Parent*

July 4

For you were called to freedom, brothers and sisters; only do not use your freedom as an opportunity for self-indulgence, but through love become slaves to one another.

Galatians 5:13

Lord, we pray for the power to be gentle; the strength to be forgiving; the patience to be understanding; and the endurance to accept the consequences of holding to what we believe to be right.

—Week of Prayer for World Peace

Take a solemn family vow to work for freedoms, large and small. And be wise, kind, and brave in the doing.

July 5

Father, how do I guard my children against being selfish and always wanting their own way? At times I can't believe these are my offspring. I have treated them with love and respect, yet they persist in their stubbornness. Is this just a phase? Have I given too much and not expected enough of them?

Is this a reflection of myself when I rebel against you, Lord? You give me everything I need, yet often I insist on "doing my own thing." But you always draw me back to your loving arms, to seek your forgiveness and your wisdom. Draw my children back, O Lord, to the circle of your love.

July 6

Unless the Lord builds the house, those who build it labor in vain.

Psalm 127:1

Home is the one place in this world where hearts are sure of each other. It is the place of confidence. It is the place where we tear off that mask of guarded and suspicious coldness which the world forces us to wear in self-defense, and where we pour out the unreserved communications of full and confiding hearts. It is the spot where expressions of tenderness gush out without any sensation of awkwardness and without any dread of ridicule.

—James L. Christensen,
New Ways to Worship

*More than bricks and mortar, O God our shelter,
this home stands on you as the foundation,
giving all who live here a refuge not only for the body
but also for the mind and the soul.*

July 7

God has brought me laughter.

Genesis 21:6 NIV

Better to laugh than cry over spilled milk,
God of chuckles and belly laughs, for it
happens a lot with kids. Thank you for the gift of
laughter. It's one kids understand—giggles are on
infant lips before words! Chuckle along at our next
blunder, so that, God help me, I'll be first to laugh.

*A healthy way to meet stress is a chuckle a day!
Looking for the lighter side helps me see around the
potholes of life to the humor possible in most anything.*

July 8

Is any thing too hard for the Lord?

Genesis 18:14 KJV

Father, somewhere I read that "attitude is everything." I am beginning to see the truth of that saying in my own children. One has the "I can" spirit and is always ready to meet challenges. It is the child who says "I can't" and will not try that I am concerned about, Lord.

My heart knows that with you all things are possible. Help me to radiate that positive attitude, so each of my children can reflect the confidence I have in you.

Hide within each timid heart the words and knowledge: "With God's help, I can."

The difference between the person who conquers a problem and the one who is conquered by it is a positive attitude.

July 9

My presence will go with you, and I will give you rest.

Exodus 33:14

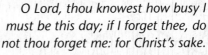

t's late at night, and still there is much to do.
Yet there is peace, holding on to a childlike
trust that God is an ever-present companion, showing
us how not to worry needlessly,
burning the candle at both ends.

O Lord, thou knowest how busy I
must be this day; if I forget thee, do
not thou forget me: for Christ's sake.

—Sir Jacob Astley

July 10

Thank you, God, for such a wonderful role model as the mother of Jesus. So often we sanitize her life, forgetting she was a courageous, creative lady who loved with heart and hand and whose example I pledge to follow.

Look beyond the portrait of Mary, pictured sweetly in a blue gown with a golden-haloed smile, and envision Mary as a mother who patched her son's robe, fixed his favorite foods, and went about her life while supporting him from the sidelines. God gives us the wisdom to go and do likewise.

July 11

So that I may walk before God in the light of life.

Psalm 56:13

I am touched to the core
with a presence I cannot explain
A loving plan enfolds me
Someone is always believing in me
calling me forth, calling me on
I am standing in grace
filled with mystery
touched with the eternal
I cannot get away from goodness
I think we name you, God.

—Macrina Wiederkehr, Seasons of Your Heart

*Human felicity is produced not so much by
great pieces of good fortune that seldom happen,
as by little advantages that occur every day.*

—Benjamin Franklin

July 12

But when in their distress they turned to the Lord, the God of Israel, and sought him, he was found by them.

2 Chronicles 15:4

t's amazing, steadfast God, how much better I feel after sharing with you even the smallest doubt or little niggling worry about being the best mom I can be. Connected, we can do great things. Alone, I am the victim of my own fears.

No matter the worries I have, small or large, you, O God, are there ahead of me with promises of help and support that relieve me and free me from getting stuck in the mire of my fears. Oh, how grateful I am.

July 13

All scripture is inspired by God and is useful for teaching…
so that everyone who belongs to God may be proficient,
equipped for every good work.

2 Timothy 3:16–17

By the reading of the Scripture, I am so renewed that all nature seems renewed around and with me. The sky seems a purer, a cooler blue, the trees a deeper green, light is sharper on the outlines of the forest, and the hills and the whole world is charged with the glory of God.

—Thomas Merton, *The Sign of Jonas*

How we love a good story, O Divine Love.
Especially a story with hope and promise and a good ending.
When it comes to your Book, give me an open ear so
that I might hear your good news, an open mind
ready to accept it, and an open heart willing
to be transformed by your love and acceptance of me.

July 14

The Father is a merciful God, who always gives us comfort.
He comforts us when we are in trouble, so that we can share
that same comfort with others in trouble.

2 Corinthians 1:3–4 CEV

Father God, disappointments come to us all, but
it is particularly poignant when my children face
disappointments. I ache for them; yet there is seldom
anything I can do except comfort them.

You give comfort, too, Lord. Your
love has been my shield against the
world's harsh realities. When I am not
able to comfort my children and protect
them from disappointment, help them
find their comfort in you. And may we
all learn to pass along to others that same
comfort you have given us.

To comfort others is to take on your shoulders
a small part of their sorrow.

July 15

*Train children in the right way, and when old,
they will not stray.*

Proverbs 22:6

Being an adviser to these offspring is both exhausting and exhilarating. At times I even think myself wise, until they reject my sageness as old-fashioned. Remind me, O God of wisdom, that they are not so much rejecting my knowledge as they are entering their own new, uncharted territory. Make me wise enough to advise them that they have what it takes to enjoy the journey without me having to highlight the route for them.

*It's humbling—and exciting—to know that
God sees us worthy of setting a standard
for our children by offering options
and being strong enough to maintain them.*

July 16

Create in me a clean heart, O God,
and put a new and right spirit within me.

Psalm 51:10

It's kind of hard to think noble thoughts,
   Lord,
When I just found three-and-a-half pairs of dirty socks
   on the bathroom floor.
They know better. Goodness knows I've told them
   often enough.
Thoughtless, care-less kids.
I make excuses for them.
They're busy—paper routes, lots of homework—
And surely they deserve an occasional unscheduled
   moment.
Still, there are some things they must learn,
And picking up their dirty socks is one of them.

—Jo Carr and Imogene Sorley

Who ran to help me when I fell,
And would some pretty story tell,
Or kiss the place to make it well?
My mother.

—Jane Taylor

July 17

*Little children, let us love, not in word or speech,
but in truth and action.*

1 John 3:18

Loving God, sometimes I
think the children vie with
each other to see who can display
the worst behavior. That's why it's
such an uphill battle to teach our
kids good manners. We want them
to know that love and rudeness
don't mix, Lord. Please help us to
show them how much more
pleasant life can be when we treat each other
with respect.

*Feel honored, humbled, too, to be the first
teacher of the lesson about "faith in action."
Even children can help—first of all by
simply being kind to one another.*

July 18

For the Lord will be your confidence.

Proverbs 3:26

O God of peace,
Who has taught us
that in returning
and rest
we shall be saved,
in quietness
and in confidence
shall be our strength:
By the might of Your
Spirit
lift us, we pray,
to Your presence,
where we may be still
and know
that You are God.
Amen.

—Diane Boice Fillmore, *Glimpses of God*

No circumstance, no person, can change Him. He is. He is with us always. And He is eternally committed to you and to me. Everything we need or long for is contained in His everlasting commitment to us. That, now and in the end, is what really matters.

—Eugenia Price, *What Really Matters*

July 19

I will both lie down and sleep in peace; for you alone, O Lord, make me lie down in safety.

Psalm 4:8

Lord, why is it that when I am the most tired or crave sleep myself, the children's bedtime becomes prolonged and difficult? There is always one last drink of water, one final trip to the bathroom, one more bedtime story, or one more postscript to the prayer. By then, desperation sets in, and my temper becomes short.

God of peace, help me to face bedtime more calmly. Help me to discover strategies for helping my children to wind down and relax. Prevent me from losing my temper, and grant me a soothing manner so the children's last memories of the day are pleasant and loving. Thank you, Lord, for your promise of a safe and peaceful sleep.

Gather all your cares and woes into a big pile, then sleep on it.

July 20

*Do not worry about anything, but in everything by prayer
and supplication with thanksgiving let your requests be made known
to God. And the peace of God, which surpasses all understanding,
will guard your hearts and your minds in Christ Jesus.*

Philippians 4:6–7

Today I am a new person. I relax and free my thoughts of every sense of pressure. No person, place or thing irritate or annoy me. I am at peace. I am a free person living in a world that is a reflection of my own love and understanding. I am not against anything. I am for everything that will improve the quality of my life. I use my words and my thoughts as tools to shape my future. I express gratitude and thanksgiving often and look for things to be thankful for. I am relaxed. I live a peaceful life.

—Louise L. Hay

July 21

So then, putting away falsehood, let all of us speak the truth to our neighbors, for we are members of one another.

Ephesians 4:25

Father, it is important to us that our children be honest with us and not try to deceive us. We have brought up all of our children to love you, Lord. We want each of them to develop a godly character, fit for a child of the King.

Walk with us and guide us as we encourage our children to be truthful. Keep the lines of communication open between us so they won't feel the need for falsehood. When a lapse occurs, put forgiveness in our hearts so we can put the incident behind us and help our children walk in truth once more.

Lies are often the wishes of a frightened heart.

July 22

I said, "I am lost." I called on your name, O Lord . . . you heard my plea.

Lamentations 3:54–56

I come humbly before you, dear Lord Jesus, confessing my lukewarm faith. Please renew my passion to serve you and trust in your merciful love for me. Thank you for always listening to me. Help me to always listen to you. Amen.

When straying from God, it's reassuring to know there is no distance so great that can't be bridged. What a marvelous, firsthand lesson to pass on to the children.

July 23

O God, I hardly have a moment to myself. As I get...the children bathed and clad and fed, the phone rings, or a neighbor calls. I can't always do what I would like to do about the house. I have the shopping to do and I take the little ones with me for an outing—and the hours fly. In no time I'm putting them to rest and planning the meal.

Help me to make this house a home, full of joy and security; a home to which we will all be eager to return at the day's end, a centre of understanding and love.

—Rita Snowden

You really need to have your own time. The problem is that even if you realize you need the time, you know you have to take it away from somebody else, and then you don't. You never say, "No." That is the fallacy of motherhood.

—Frances Wells Burck

July 24

Without wood a fire goes out; without gossip a quarrel dies down.

Proverbs 26:20 NIV

Gossip hurts, Lord. Even children aren't immune to gossip. One is called names, one may be physically intimidated, and another is ostracized because of false information.

Though it's sometimes tempting to pass on juicy morsels, help me to guard my lips and resist the temptation to fuel the fire of gossip.

Impress upon my youngsters the harm and danger involved in spreading stories that may not be true, and spare them from becoming victims of gossip. May our tongues be used to praise and not condemn.

To reject gossip is to put out a fire before it starts.

July 25

Cast all your anxiety on him, because he cares for you.

1 Peter 5:7

Lord, in this frenzied puttering about the house, see more! The dusting, straightening, muttering, are but the poor efforts of a heavy heart to help time pass. Praying on my knees I get uptight; for hearts and lives are not the only things that need to be put right. And, while I clean, please, if tears should fall, they're settling the dust—that's all. Lord, I will straighten all I can and You take over what we mothers cannot do.

—Ruth Bell Graham, *Prodigals and Those Who Love Them*

Since God is in control of the minute details of life, you can relax, knowing that He will reveal His plan for your life step by step.

—Ray Pritchard, *The Road Best Traveled*

July 26

Consider it pure joy . . . whenever you face trials of many kinds, because you know that the testing of your faith produces perseverance.

James 1:2–3 NIV

As the children encounter the rough places of life, Lord, may I find wisdom to help them turn those places into something better. Just as an oyster uses a grain of sand to make a beautiful pearl, please continue to inspire us, O God, to find the positive in every situation.

Dear God,

As I rise each day, give me the strength, courage, and patience to do the best I can for my family. All through the day, guide me with your grace and divine direction into right action and right decision. And when the day is done and it is time for me to rest my weary mind and body, take the burden of my troubles from me so that I can sleep. Watch over me and mine throughout the night, and when it is time to arise to a new day, be there for me all over again. Amen.

Life becomes much easier and more enjoyable
when we know we are never alone.
We always have God to turn to for strength, hope,
guidance, and renewal. He is on the job 24 hours a day,
7 days a week, 365 days a year.

July 28

He gives power to the faint, and strengthens the powerless.

Isaiah 40:29

A question for you, wise God: Whom do I mother first, my aging parents or my children? I'm pulled like a wishbone as I straddle generations, mother to all. Feeding, cleaning, chasing, lullabying. Keep me strong. Inspire solutions that include even the littlest kids helping out, for it takes a village to tend to everyone.

God gives the shoulder according to the burden.

—German Proverb

July 29

Father, when I hold my tiny baby in my arms, I can't even imagine future teenage rebellion in my own home, angry words and accusations surrounding us, and our own child testing us at every turn. But it happens. When it does, we'll need your strength and confidence to help us weather the storm. We'll need the safety of your arms to gather up our courage and your wisdom to contain the damage caused by hateful words.

We gratefully remember the many times you treated us with love and gave us your forgiveness when we rebelled against you. Help us to deal with our child in a loving way and to look forward with hope to the time when the storms are over.

We learn obedience through suffering.
When we have suffered enough,
God's love can win us back to him.

July 30

But if we hope for what we do not see, we wait for it with patience.

Romans 8:25

Progress, in the folds of a family, O God, is not a straight, flat line but rather a series of ups and downs. Like squiggles on a heart monitor, they merely chart the daily rhythm of life. Give me energy and patience to go with the flow.

A word of advice to mothers of kids who disobey, rebel, and test patience and values: Remain calm but resolute, for kids need the security of boundaries and consequences.

July 31

Hope does not disappoint us, because God's love has been poured into our hearts through the Holy Spirit that has been given to us.

Romans 5:5

Father, young children are filled with ideas about what they want to be when they become adults. But as they grow older, their choices narrow and become more practical. Lord, you are the Great Encourager. Fill me with your optimism so I may inspire my children to hold on to their dreams and to give wings to their goals through positive action.

Help me to feed their dreams with realistic encouragement. When the children express their own doubts, place in their hearts the knowledge that they can never discount you—that if you put the dream in their heart, you can make it come true.

Dreams are another form of hope;
and hope is God opening a door.

My Prayer Life

August 1

Let us then pursue what makes for peace and for mutual upbuilding.

Romans 14:19

Dear God,
    Drop thy still dews of quietness,
Till all our strivings cease;
Take from our souls the strain and stress,
And let our ordered lives confess
The beauty of thy peace.

—John Greenleaf Whittier

Listen. There's good news today.
God's provisions for our past
are not only sufficient,
but his promise for our future
is incredibly bright!

—Jack Hayford, *I'll Hold You in Heaven*

August 2

I planted, Apollos watered, but God gave the growth.

1 Corinthians 3:6

Creator of the earth, you are the God of sun and sky, trees and grass, fruit and flowers—the God of growing things. I offer my praise and gratitude for the quiet loveliness of my garden, where I can delight in the constant renewal of life. Help me to remember that though I plant and water, it is you who provides the life and growth.

Lord, my home is a garden, too. My children are the tender fruits and flowers you have brought into being. Teach me to nurture them lovingly and to uproot the weeds that would choke out your goodness. May these young ones be a fitting bouquet to honor you.

Children are the seeds of the future from which tomorrow's gardens will grow.

August 3

"Love your neighbor as yourself." Love does no wrong to a neighbor; therefore, love is the fulfilling of the law.

Romans 13:9–10

Lord, if only everyone could adopt your law of love as our neighbors have. I thank you for sending good friends who are always ready to provide our children with shelter and a cookie in any emergency, to lend equipment or advice, to offer an occasional ride or a meal—to help out in any way they can. Where would we be without their valued assistance?

I am grateful for their kindness, their willingness, and their generous spirits. Bless these loving people, Father, who are your hands reaching out to care for us.

Please make me a good neighbor to them, and may I find many opportunities to return your love by helping them when they are in need.

Children can bring good neighbors closer together.

August 4

Watch yourselves closely, so as neither to forget the things that your eyes have seen nor to let them slip from your mind all the days of your life; make them known to your children and your children's children.

Deuteronomy 4:9

Strengthen all that is good within us, and teach us to put it forth. Help us to restrain whatever is evil, to bind it for Christ's sake and by the power of God, through Christ Jesus given unto us. We pray that God will grant unto us, that the fountain of all goodness and divine love may be in us. May we have those secret beginnings of grace; may we learn how to chastise selfishness, how to humble pride, how to restrain every wayward and vicious inclination that offends against the purity of our souls.

—Henry Ward Beecher, *Plymouth Pulpit*

August 5

*Grandchildren are the crown of the aged,
and the glory of children is their parents.*

Proverbs 17:6

Lord God, of all the gifts you have given mothers,
grandparents top the list.

They understand the problems of being parents.

They know instinctively how to help.

They are always willing.

They love us unconditionally.

Who else would tend to us when we're sick, do the
laundry, provide meals, give free babysitting services,
and act as though we're doing them a favor?

Dear Lord, just as we don't deserve all you give us,
we can never deserve the love and devotion of loving
grandparents. But we accept their gifts with gratitude
and ask you to grant these loved ones endless joy and
blessings for their loyalty and commitment to us.

*Grandparents are a family's
most valuable natural resource.*

August 6

The Lord will guide you always.

Isaiah 58:11 NIV

Father, I abandon myself into your hands. Do with me what you will. Whatever you may do, I thank you. I am ready for all, I accept all. Let only your will be done in me, and in all your creatures, I wish no more than this, O Lord. Into your hands I commend my soul. I offer it to you, with all the love of my heart, for I love you, and so need to love you, to give myself, to surrender myself into your hands without reserve, and with boundless confidence, for you are my Father.

—Charles de Foucauld

It is today for which we are responsible.
God still owns tomorrow.

—Elisabeth Elliot, *Let Me Be a Woman*

August 7

Whoever breaks one of the least of these commandments,
and teaches others to do the same, will be called least in the kingdom
of heaven; but whoever does them and teaches them will be called great
in the kingdom of heaven.

Matthew 5:19

Lord, it is clear that you expect us to teach our children right from wrong. Your words tell us what will happen if we do not honor this commission. You clearly state we are to teach by example. It is an awesome responsibility.

Examine us, Father, and expose our own sinful behavior that presents a harmful witness to our family. Save us from envy, deceit, hate, and lust. Fill us instead with reverence, integrity, truthfulness, and love.

We want our children to walk uprightly. Make us worthy of this calling so they may enjoy your favor and honor.

If you wish to teach your children right from wrong,
give them behavior to imitate.

August 8

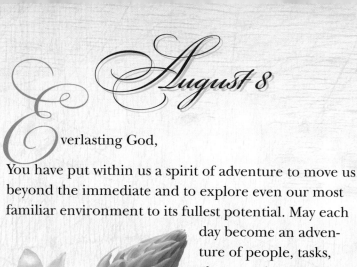

Everlasting God,

You have put within us a spirit of adventure to move us beyond the immediate and to explore even our most familiar environment to its fullest potential. May each day become an adventure of people, tasks, places, and responsibilities. And when I feel gray and lifeless, may your Spirit remind me that each day brings its own gifts and that the best is yet to be.

Hope for tomorrow must be there,
but the focus of attention must be on today.
Yesterday is gone; tomorrow is not yet ours.

—Jan Markell, *Waiting for a Miracle*

August 9

She looks well to the ways of her household,
and does not eat the bread of idleness.

Proverbs 31:27

I confess, Lord, I hate housework! Doing the same tasks over and over does not thrill me. But I love seeing my family in clean clothes, and I love to inhale the fragrance of clean sheets and towels, so I gladly do the laundry.

I hate housework, but I love guarding my family from germs that cause illness, so I willingly wash dishes, scrub floors and bathrooms, dust, and vacuum.

I hate housework, but I love having my family live in an uncluttered environment, so I happily pick up the day's accumulation of "things" and trot them back to the places they belong.

I may hate housework, Lord, but I love my family, so I do it anyway. Thank you, Father, for giving me a house to clean and a family to care for.

Home is the place where the humblest actions
are done willingly, out of love.

August 10

Perfect love casts out fear.

1 John 4:18

I am not sure I understand how perfect your love for me is, Father, but I do know that it is better than I can possibly imagine. My fears, and I do have several, have no place when I allow your love to govern and guide me. Every trace of terror is gone when I think of being under your watchful care. Thank you for the peace and security that truth brings and help me to apply it daily. When fear arises, may it drive me into your love and so make me more dependent on you and less susceptible to the "what ifs" of life.

—Charles Stanley, *A Touch of His Peace*

August 11

You hem me in, behind and before, and lay your hand upon me.

Psalm 139:5

O Lord, seek us, O Lord, find us
   In Thy patient care;
Be Thy love before, behind us,
Round us, everywhere:
Lest the god of this world blind us,
Lest he speak us fair,
Lest he forge a chain to bind us,
Lest he bait a snare.
   Turn not from us, call to mind us,
   Find, embrace us, bear;
   Be Thy Love before, behind us,
   Round us, everywhere.

—Christina Rossetti,
"The World. Self-destruction"

A babe is a mothers's anchor.
She cannot swing far from her moorings.

—Henry Ward Beecher, *Life Thoughts*

August 12

On this doorstep I stand
        year after year
and watch you going
and think: may you not
skin your knees. May you
not catch your fingers
in car doors. May
your hearts not break.
May tide and weather
wait for your coming
and may you grow strong
to break
all webs of my weaving.

—Evangeline Paterson

August 13

Show me your ways, O Lord, teach me your paths.
Guide me in your truth and teach me, for you are God my Savior,
and my hope is in you all day long.

Psalm 25:4–5 NIV

Mothering is a curious relationship, Lord. It requires that I love my children intensely, but at the same time I am pulling them closer, I must prepare to push them from the nest. How do I find the proper balance between pushing and pulling?

You are my parent, Lord. Though I am a mother, I am also your child. Be with me as I travel this path. Lead me with a steady hand as I walk the fine line between nurturing and letting go. When I can no longer walk beside my children, please give them your hand to guide and protect them.

I pray that though they outgrow my mothering, my children will never outgrow my love for them.

Motherhood is a continuous balancing act
between giving too much and giving too little.

August 14

*To one he gave five talents, to another two, to another one,
to each according to his ability.*

Matthew 25:15

Inspired by you, Great God, and grateful for
the unique gifts we're discovering, we toss
ourselves into the stream of life to make ripples wherever we are. In your hands, our gifts can offer a gift
that keeps on making ever-widening circles to reach all
those stranded on shore.

*Character, that sublime health
which values one moment as another,
and makes us great in all conditions.*

—Ralph Waldo Emerson

August 15

From childhood you have known the sacred writings that are able to instruct you for salvation through faith in Christ Jesus.

2 Timothy 3:15

Scooting over to make room, God of daily bread, the kids and I greet you over our peanut butter and jelly lunch. Through simple graces and verses to bless childhood fare and bedtime prayers to offer you the day, I'm honored to introduce you to my child.

*When worrying about
what to lay as foundations
for all the children need to know,
think first of the timeless blueprint
of verse and prayer.*

August 16

Creator God, I've been so busy being a mother, I've neglected my own creativity. I thought it was the right thing to do, but lately I've felt the urge to stretch my talents.

Lord, please guide me. I feel guilty about wanting to do something for myself, but I think this will reduce my stress, and my spirit could use a little uplifting!

You have given me many talents. Can I use them to renew my mind and spirit?

Your creativity in forming our world serves as my daily inspiration. Take away my feelings of guilt, and replace them with wondrous ideas that will lift me up *and* serve you. Amen.

When you're running on empty,
pull over and let God fill your tank.

August 17

I t is so easy to become overwhelmed, faithful Lord, by the needs surrounding us. Our voices join with the faithful through the centuries who have pleaded for the coming of your kingdom, for an end to the violence and suffering. We have prayed for restitution and justice to overcome deceit and despair. Give us strength to continue to do our part, courage to stand apart, and compassion to reach out to those who have been torn apart by their life experiences. Help us change the world with you, one moment at a time.

Whatever tests in life you're facing, whether it's a challenge of relationships, finances, or your career, the loving God who created you is always available to guide you into a better life.

August 18

I will seek the lost, and I will bring back the strayed,
and I will bind up the injured, and I will strengthen the weak.

Grace of my heart, I turn to you when I am
feeling lost and alone. You restore me, O God,
with strength and hope and the courage to face a new
day. You bless me with joys, and comfort me through
trials and tribulations. You direct my thoughts, guide
my actions, temper my words. You give me the patience
and kindness I need to be a good wife, mother, friend.
Grace of my heart, I turn to you.

Each of us can turn within to connect
with an amazing place full of amazing grace.
This is where God lives. This is where we live.
This is our soul.

August 19

How very good and pleasant it is when kindred live together in unity!

Psalm 133:1

Lord, it nearly drives me to distraction to hear my children arguing over trifles. Each wants what the other has. When one says something, the other contradicts. I try, but there seems to be no way to avoid these battles.

I need your steadying hand, Father, to help me cope. Only you can calm the waters of discontent that swirl around them and plant peace within their hearts.

Soothe us with the balm of your Holy Spirit so my children can live together in pleasant harmony.

Don't worry about your children's disagreements.
It takes rough edges tumbling together
to polish the most beautiful stones.

August 20

Clap your hands. . . shout to God with loud songs of joy.

Psalm 47:1

Help me listen between the beats of my headache to hear hearts overflowing with enthusiasm and joy. Join our parade, God of music and motion; it's simple, but it's in your honor. Let us all make a "noiseful" joy.

Children are born noisy,
something that takes getting used to.
And yet, how often sheer delight in the moment
underlies each squeal, each shout,
each clanging-banging moment of play.
May we join in.

August 21

God, when my child looks at me with trusting
eyes, it gives me a sense of the incredible power
I have in that small person's life. Give me the guidance
and the wisdom to never take advantage of that gift.
May I never treat my child with less respect than I
would treat myself. And grant that if I do falter and
use this special life for my own gain, that you would
humble me with the realization that parenting is not
about cloning but about creating unique persons.

I promise. . .
not to live through you, sweet child,
and
not to make you do something just because I can
and
not to reload the dishwasher after you help
and
not to call you from play until supper is really ready
and
to give myself time-outs when I'm cranky
and
to understand and guide you when you are.

August 22

Glorify God in your body, and in your spirit.

1 Corinthians 6:20 KJV

Lord, mothers always worry about their children's health yet often neglect their own. I plead guilty. Too much anxiety, too little sleep, too little time for trips to the doctor all take their toll on my body and leave me open to illness.

I owe it to my family, Lord, to stay healthy. They depend on me for so many things that my illness would put a strain on them. Please help me to be sensible: to get enough rest, cut down on stress, and seek medical help when needed.

Most of all, I need your healing spirit to touch me as I come to you in prayer, so I may continue to honor you through service to my family.

Good health is a treasure. Spend it wisely.

August 23

I can look over my shoulder and see times when you, Pathfinding God, were a ready and dependable companion. I couldn't have done it without you. And I believe that you are already waiting to take my hand into tomorrow—knowledge that gives me the security to risk.

But God requires our trust in order to keep us from hindering His answer to our prayer by our own restless activity or flight. When we ask God to do anything for us, we must give Him time to do it, and carefully avoid rushing off in unbelieving haste to do something that would probably quite hinder His plan.

—A. B. Simpson, *The Life of Prayer*

August 24

All things work together for good for those who love God.

Romans 8:28

Who would've thought it, Lord, that from confusion and disarray while shopping with the children; cooking another breakfast, lunch, and dinner; or getting the kids settled in bed that such wisdom and discovery could come. Thank you for the gift of perseverance that let me see it through.

There is much in life that seems meaningless. And then, when I can see no evidence of meaning, some glimpse is given which reveals the strange weaving of purposefulness and beauty.

—Madeleine L'Engle, Glimpses of Grace

August 25

The godly are able to be generous with their gifts and loans to others, and their children are a blessing.

Psalm 37:26 LB

God, I thank you for my children. Please be with them today in all their coming and going and in all their thinking and doing.

—Marian Wright Edelman, *Guide My Feet*

Encourage your child to learn, to master, to question—to try. It may feel like a big adventure and maybe even a huge risk, but you can relax, knowing that God is blessing the undertaking and providing the fuel for the journey.

August 26

Do your own work well, and then you will have something to be proud of.
Don't compare yourself with others. We each must carry our own load.

Galatians 6:4–5 CEV

Lord, it is so hard to build a sense of responsibility in some children. Each child reacts so differently to chores. One gets them done right away with no grumbling, while another dawdles and accomplishes nothing. I don't want to be just a scorekeeper, keeping track of who does what. I want my children to learn the value of carrying part of the responsibility for our family's comfort.

Give me the wisdom to develop in each child a healthy respect for their work and for the way it fits into a larger plan for the good of all. You value work, Lord. Instill in my kids a desire to carry part of the load and to feel pride in the accomplishment.

Responsibility is growth;
it is its own reward.

August 27

Whatever is true, whatever is honorable, whatever is just,
whatever is pure, whatever is pleasing, whatever is commendable,
if there is any excellence and if there is anything worthy of praise,
think about these things.

Philippians 4:8–9

Help me see the connection between our relationship, O God, and the ones I have with others: my spouse, my friends, but especially the children. I use them all as excuses for not praying when they're a prime reason to pray! Hear me now.

Oh, what peace we often forfeit,
Oh, what needless pain we bear,
All because we do not carry
Everything to God in prayer!

—Joseph Scriven

August 28

Do not repay evil for evil or abuse for abuse; but, on the contrary, repay with a blessing. It is for this that you were called— that you might inherit a blessing.

1 Peter 3:9

Even if my motives are pure, O God, I need to step back and let you guide—all of us—instead of trying to control. Often my mouth is open before I think. Keep me quiet for the sake of peace and learning.

May I not vainly hurt the feelings of my children. Forbid that I should laugh at their mistakes or resort to shame and ridicule as punishment.

—James L. Christensen,
Creative Ways to Worship

August 29

The Lord will guide you continually,
and satisfy your needs in parched places.

Isaiah 58:11

O may thy spirit guide my feet
   In ways of righteousness;
Make every path of duty straight,
And plain before my face.
Amen.

—Joachim Neander

Like toddlers, we take a few small steps forward each day and
try to relish the moments. By focusing on one day at a time,
we can eventually look back and be amazed at how far we've
come, guided as we were by an open-handed God.

August 30

Let my teaching fall like rain and my words descend like dew,
like showers on new grass, like abundant rain on tender plants.
I will proclaim the name of the Lord.

Deuteronomy 32:2–3 NIV

Heavenly Father, talking to others about
you isn't always easy. It's hard for me to
express my emotions in mere words. Though I long to
tell my children all you mean to
me, self-consciousness gets in
the way. Help me to speak to
them from my heart. Inspire me
with language that will fall on
fertile soil.

Lord, may I be like Moses as I
teach my children about you,
with words as welcome as the
rain and dew on thirsty plants.

Planting God's Word in a child's heart
will yield an abundant garden.

August 31

You see that faith was active along with his works,
and faith was brought to completion by the works.

ear Lord,

Teach my children to follow my lead in actions and deeds and to model my behavior more so than my words. Often I speak in frustration, but help me to always act in patience, kindness, and love. I want the same for my children. Help them do as I do, not as I say. Help my husband see beyond my occasional sharp or impatient words, my words of confusion, fear, and annoyance when things aren't going the way I would like. Help him to see the love I give, the work I do, the way I live and move and have my being. Amen.

Affirm:
My thoughts and ideas are fresh;
My words are thoughtful and loving;
My actions are helpful and caring.

My Prayer Life

_____

_____

_____

_____

_____

_____

_____

_____

_____

_____

_____

_____

September 1

Your word is a lamp to my feet and a light to my path. I have sworn an oath and confirmed it, to observe your righteous ordinances.

Psalm 119:105–106

Heavenly Father, your words have been a beacon on my life's journey, and your love, my lifeline. My children, too, have been surrounded by your word since they were infants. They have never doubted your wisdom.

But soon the world will creep in and your values will be questioned. I dread to hear the words coming from my children's mouths: "Everybody's doing it; why can't I?"

Lord, you are the God of all that is good. Help me to be firm yet fair when these situations occur. Surround my children with your love, and open their eyes to your truth. Insulate them from the pressures that would weaken our family's witness to the world.

When deciding what is right,
use God's yardstick.

September 2

May you have peace—
    Not of the stagnant pool, but of deep
waters, flowing.
May you have poise—
Not of the sheltered tree, but of the oak, deep rooted,
    storm strengthened, and free.
May you have power—
Not of fisted might, but of the quickened seed
    stretching toward infinite light.
Amen.

—James L. Christensen, *New Ways to Worship*

Share looks of love over the heads of the children,
for they need to see how partners, lovers,
friends, and mates joined by God stay
connected to him and one another.
It's a quiet lesson that will benefit
them for the rest of their lives.

September 3

God has given each of you some special abilities; be sure to use them to help each other, passing on to others God's many kinds of blessings.

1 Peter 4:10 LB

God of justice, we confess that we are too quick
at times to judge those around us, basing our
opinions not upon what is written in their hearts but
what is easily seen by our lazy eyes.
Keep us faithful to challenge one
another any time we find ourselves
speaking in generalities about any
group of people or repeating jokes and
slurs that offend and degrade. Remind us
that all of creation bears the imprint of
your face, all people are children of yours,
all souls are illuminated by your divine
spark. We know that whatever diminishes
others diminishes your spirit at work in
them. Make us respectful, humble, and
open to the diversity around us
that reflects your divine imagination
and creativity.

September 4

Draw near to God, and he will draw near to you.

James 4:8

Though long the weary way we tread,
And sorrow crown each lingering year,
No path we shun, no darkness dread,
Our hearts still whispering, thou art near!

—Oliver Wendell Holmes, "Hymn of Trust"

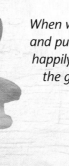

*When we humble ourselves like little children
and put on no airs of self-sufficiency, but run
happily into the joy of our Father's embrace,
the glory of his grace is magnified and the
longing of our soul is satisfied.*

—John Piper, *Desiring God*

September 5

By this I know that you are pleased with me; because my enemy has not triumphed over me. But you have upheld me because of my integrity, and set me in your presence forever.

Psalm 41:11–12

God, it's that time again, when my children are off to school; when my house becomes a little less noisy and my life becomes a little less hectic. I will miss them, but I will also cherish this time for me. Time to work on my own life, time to follow my own dreams, time to listen to the prompting of my own inner voice. As the days grow shorter outside, let me make use of my time in the highest and best ways. Let me be me for a while, until they all come back home again. Amen!

Each part of a mother's day is meant to be savored. For what good is a life if we cannot enjoy where we are on the way to where we're going?

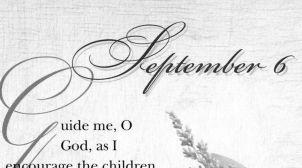

September 6

Guide me, O God, as I encourage the children to be positive—to see the good in each day—each person in their classrooms, new friends, each challenge. Hope and optimism are gifts from your hand that can guide them for life.

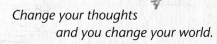

Change your thoughts and you change your world.

—Norman Vincent Peale

September 7

I sought the Lord, and he answered me,
and delivered me from all my fears.

Psalm 34:4

hen we are in fear and despair, help us to remember that You, Jesus, have given us the victory in advance, and we are bound to win the battle we face.... Our fears are the result of not trusting fully in You. Make us see the foolishness of fearing. Turn our eyes in the right direction unto You, Lord, and away from the waves.

—Corrie ten Boom, *Each New Day*

Cast aside thy questionings.
Fling aside thy fears.

—Frances J. Roberts, *Come Away My Beloved*

September 8

"Come and hear what the word is that comes from the Lord." They come to you . . . and they hear your words . . . but their heart is set on their gain.

Ezekiel 33:30–31

Children spot phonies a mile away, Lord. Please keep me from saying one thing and doing another—like saying we are to love others, even those who are different, but turning away from or ridiculing such people when I come face-to-face. Keep me authentic.

If we do not have love in our hearts, our words of love will have little meaning. If we do not truly enjoy our faith, nobody is going to catch the fire of enjoyment from us.

—Madeleine L'Engle,
Glimpses of Grace

September 9

I . . . beg you to lead a life worthy of the calling to which you have been called, with all humility and gentleness, with patience, bearing with one another in love.

Ephesians 4:1–2

Lord, I am in urgent need of an extra dose of patience with my children. Sometimes I think I cannot bear another whine, another scream, another temper tantrum. My nerves are worn thin, and I am tempted to react in kind.

How I would like to be able to handle each situation calmly! But I am not perfect, and what I want to do, I cannot do without your help.

Father, guide me daily. You are a God of infinite kindness and patience. Let the waves of your love wash over me. When rough times occur, enable me to keep the children's behavior in perspective, and let me look at their undesirable actions through eyes filtered by your love. Help me deal with them in an effective way, one that is acceptable to you.

September 10

I need Thee ev'ry hour, most gracious Lord;
    No tender voice like Thine can peace afford.
I need Thee ev'ry hour, stay Thou near by;
Temptations lose their pow'r when Thou art nigh.
I need Thee ev'ry hour, in joy or pain;
Come quickly and abide, or life is vain.
I need Thee ev'ry hour, teach me Thy will;
And Thy rich promises in me fulfill.
I need Thee ev'ry hour, most Holy One
O make me Thine indeed, Thou blessed Son.
I need Thee, O I need Thee;
Ev'ry hour I need Thee!
O bless me now, My Savior, I come to Thee.
Amen.

—Annie S. Hawks

*Stay on your knees. And hang on to your faith
like a life preserver! The Lord is at work
in the lives of your children,
even though you see no evidence of it
at the moment.*

—Dr. James Dobson, *Solid Answers*

September 11

here they go, O God. Out of my arms and into their world. Steady me as I pause at each threshold. I dare only follow at a distance lest they see me hovering and think they can't do it alone. Or, worse, that I can't. Help me find ways to show I know we both can.

There they go.
Stroller, trike, bike, car, jet,
train, moving van. When
each need arises, God can
help reinvent those left
behind as new creations:
long-distance mothers.

September 12

You visit the earth and water it, you greatly enrich it.

Psalm 65:9

Dear God, show us ways we can help your hurting, needful world. Our children need to see that we are not helpless or hopeless but that all efforts, small as they might seem, can matter. Your world could use a creative kind of mothering.

Mothers should run the world! Who better to get a lot done? And with good stewardship. Like piecing together a quilt of leftovers, rescuing birds, or forging truces, mothers tend to think "preserve and create" rather than "throw away and fight."

September 13

So I tell you, whatever you ask for in prayer, believe that you have received it, and it will be yours.

Mark 11:24

Before prayer
I weave a silence on my lips,
I weave a silence into my mind,
I weave a silence within my heart.
I close my ears to distractions,
I close my eyes to attentions,
I close my heart to temptations.
Calm me O Lord as you stilled the storm,
Still me O Lord, keep me from harm.
Let all the tumult within me cease,
Enfold me Lord in your peace.

—Traditional Celtic prayer

Toss prayers aloft and hear God speak in the voice of nature;
see God as a companion in the face and hand of a friend;
feel God as red, red rose and believe. Do not be in a hurry
to fill up an empty space with words and embellishments,
before it has been filled with a deep interior space.

—Father Alexander Elchaninov

September 14

One generation shall laud your works to another,
and shall declare your mighty acts.

Psalm 145:4

Keep us connected, O God of all time, to those who've come before. Inspire us to tell family tales and to pull out family albums and family Bibles and handed-down antiques to show the connecting links of which your love forges us into a whole.

Embrace change, for "new-fashioned" will become old-fashioned soon enough. Each generation is on its own cutting edge, and today is as good as yesterday was for our ancestors.

September 15

*Now I know only in part; then I will know fully,
even as I have been fully known. And now faith, hope, and love abide,
these three; and the greatest of these is love.*

1 Corinthians 13:12–13

Lord, give me faith that tries and tests the things
unseen, and assures itself of thee who
art the truth, that doubt may not overwhelm,
nor darkness cover me; give me hope,
that I may follow the light of thy sure
promises, and lose not the way nor
fall into byways; give me love, that I
may give thee myself as thou givest; for
thou, O Lord God, art the thing that I long for;
and thou art blessedness beyond all thought and
heart's desiring.

—Frederick MacNutt

September 16

I will give you the treasures of darkness.

My guard is constant and vigilant, protecting me against the next episode of my humanness. I know to err is human, but why so often? Peace only comes, God of wholeness, through reassurance that with you, mistakes, errors—even disasters—can yield treasures. I am so grateful.

Things get broken, plans change. And in God's grace, mothers are good at contingency plans. So are kids. Making something useless into useful is a lesson they grasp. They love nothing better than cutting, pasting, and gluing back together.

September 17

He took them up in his arms, laid his hands on them, and blessed them.

Mark 10:16

Bless my child, O God, who is...
milk mustaches, snaggletoothed grins,
Let the little children come...
tree climber, sand pile architect, chef, and inventor,
Forbid none of them, even...
neon-haired teen with enough pierced body parts to
    look like fishing lures in a bass
This child, too, a beloved renegade who makes me
    smile as well as...
student, cocky and shy, foolish and wise
Seeking my plan, my will by daring to search, dream...
grown-up visionary and doer
Using my gifts to build a new world, a better way.
This is our child, a blessing to us both.
Amen.

September 18

And God saw every thing that he had made,
and, behold, it was very good.

Genesis 1:31 KJV

Heavenly Father, when you made the earth, you were satisfied with the job and pronounced it "good." Because I am your child, I find satisfaction in creating, too. I give you thanks, Father, for the gift of creativity. Help me never to discourage but to encourage the sparks of creativity in my children, so they can experience the pleasure of struggle and fulfillment in making something new. Only you can satisfy our longing souls by filling them with creative achievement.

In creating something new, we are reborn.
With each creation we become a new person.

September 19

The meek will be filled with fresh joy from the Lord,
and the poor shall exult in the Holy One of Israel.
Bullies will vanish and scoffers will cease.

Isaiah 29:19–20 LB

Lord, teach us to forgive:
        to look deep into the hearts
of those who wound us,
so that we may glimpse,
in that dark, still water,
not just the reflection
of our own face
but yours as well.

—Sheila Cassidy

September 20

But store up for yourselves treasures in heaven, where neither moth
nor rust consumes and where thieves do not break in and steal.
For where your treasure is, there your heart will be also.

Matthew 6:20–21

O Lord of Heav'n and earth, and sea,
　　To Thee all praise and glory be;
How shall we show our love to Thee, Who givest all?
The golden sunshine, vernal air,
Sweet flowers and fruit, Thy love declare;
When harvest ripens, Thou art there, Who givest all.
For peaceful homes, and healthful days,
For all the blessings earth displays,
We owe Thee thankfulness and praise, Who givest all.

—*The Book of Common Prayer*

September 21

So we do not lose heart. Even though our outer nature is wasting away,
our inner nature is being renewed day by day.

2 Corinthians 4:16

Holy Spirit,

I seek your wisdom and strength so that
I can adapt to the changes of each new season. As the
days grow shorter and the nights longer, as the warm
winds give way to cool, crisp breezes, as the leaves on
the trees explode in bold color, so will I give way to
changes. Help me to adapt, to bend, to be flexible
so that I can continue to function at my best on the
inside, despite the changes going on outside of me.
And as the darker days of winter loom near, let my
heart be filled with only love and light and warmth for
myself and for my family. Amen.

As the seasons change and the exterior world
becomes a different place, we can find the courage
and power and guidance we need by staying focused
on the unchangeable, unmovable, infinite center within.

September 22

Everyone then who hears these words of mine and acts on them will be like a wise man who built his house on rock. The rain fell, the floods came, and the winds blew and beat on that house, but it did not fall, because it had been founded on rock.

Matthew 7:24–25

God, help me be honest so my children will learn honesty. Help me be kind so my children will learn kindness. Help me be faithful so my children will learn faith. Help me love so my children will be loving.

—Marian Wright Edelman, *Guide My Feet*

*More than a place,
a love-built home
is where the heart dwells.*

September 23

*Like sheep you wandered away from God, but now you have returned
to your Shepherd, the Guardian of your souls
who keeps you safe from all attacks.*

1 Peter 2:25 LB

Keep me at evening,
Keep me at morning,
Keep me at noon,
I am tired,
astray and stumbling, shield me from sin.

—Traditional Celtic prayer

*I can't count the days since I last prayed
much less considered God's ideas about
what I'm doing. I've been too busy... until I
realized I was losing my cool with regularity
and acting entirely too big for my shoes!*

September 24

When you send forth your spirit, they are created;
and you renew the face of the ground.

Psalm 104:30

The blessings of the fall season are abundant. Children go back to school, giving a mother time to herself. The holidays are coming, with all the related excitement, but are still far enough away to plan for. The air grows crisp and out come the sweaters and long pants.
Tree branches burst forth in gold and red and yellow, illuminating the landscape. Night skies are clearer and stars shine

brighter as the full harvest moon rises over the hill. This is a time for turning inward, for slowing down the pace of life and learning to savor the sweet sights and sounds and smells of each and every moment.

September 25

In all things we are more than conquerors through him who loved us.

Romans 8:37

Lord...Please show me in some small way that You care about us. Speak to me, Lord, so that I have the assurance that You haven't forgotten us and left us alone. I need to know that somehow You are going to "work all things for our good."

—Lillian Sparks, *Parents Cry Too!*

Hope is always of God;
hopelessness is always of evil.
Faith is always right;
fear and despair are always wrong.
We can rest on the love of God,
knowing that His love for us
boundlessly surpasses our own.

—Catherine Marshall, *Beyond Ourselves*

September 26

Commit your work to the Lord, and your plans will be established.

Proverbs 16:3

Lord, each day we wage the homework battle at our house. I have mixed feelings about my children's homework, Lord. I understand there is much to learn, but with hours of homework, the kids have little time for play. I am sympathetic, but since they must do the work, I want them to be thorough. They want to do just enough to "get by."

I trust you to know what is best for each of them, and I commit this problem to your care, Father. Help us to sort through the options and arrive at a good plan for all.

No problem is too big or too small for God.

September 27

You are safe in the care of the Lord your God.

1 Samuel 25:29 LB

Calm me enough, O Lord, to breathe deeply and restoratively despite my racing heart, pounding headache, and generally fatigued body and mind. Prayer restores me in the presence of all that threatens to undo me, which I name to you now.

You might breathe with a prayer or an affirmation in mind. For example, as you breathe in, say to yourself, I am. And as you breathe out, say to yourself, In God's hands.

—Alla Renée Bozarth, Ph.D., *A Journey through Grief*

September 28

My God, you have told me that you would make my family great.
So I, your servant, am brave enough to pray to you.

1 Chronicles 17:25 NCV

Dear God, from whom every family receives its true name, I pray for all the members of my family: for those who are growing up, that they may increase in wisdom and love; for those facing changes, that they may meet them with hope; for those who are weak, that they may find strength; for those with heavy burdens, that they may carry them lightly; for those who are old and frail, that they may grow in faith.

—Anonymous

Like potpourri, the unique individual "ingredients"
of a family make a wondrous mixture, stirred as it is
by God's enduring hand of possibilities.

September 29

We do not present our supplication before you on the ground of our righteousness, but on the ground of your great mercies.

Daniel 9:18

The Lord is my light and my salvation;
whom shall I fear?
The Lord is the stronghold of my life;
of whom shall I be afraid?
When evildoers assail me
to devour my flesh—
my adversaries and foes—
they shall stumble and fall.
Though an army encamp against me,
my heart shall not fear;
though war rise up against me,
yet I will be confident.

Psalm 27:1–3

September 30

Rejoice, O people of Jerusalem, rejoice in the Lord your God!...
Once more the autumn rains will come, as well as those of spring.

O God, stir new possibilities for our vibrant family into life among embers of trust in you. We know the Spirit fans the flame of growth so that we may become one with you, the root from which we, leaf and folk, have their source.

Toss a handful of leaves onto a fire, naming them as hope-filled prayers for the children who too soon will be as scattered as the beautiful swirling leaves, and know God follows each.

My Prayer Life

_____

_____

_____

_____

_____

_____

_____

_____

_____

_____

October 1

Ask, and it will be given to you; search, and you will find; knock, and the door will be opened for you. For everyone who asks receives, and everyone who searches finds, and for everyone who knocks, the door will be opened.

Matthew 7:7–8

Kids ask the most amazing questions, Wise One. Mothers are supposed to have all the answers; help me live with my ignorance. Remind me that I don't need all the answers, just a willingness to consider the questions and honor the questioners.

Ask, knock, search—imperative verbs implying God's blessing on our quests.

October 2

I will instruct you and teach you the way you should go;
I will counsel you with my eye upon you.

Psalm 32:8

Teach me Thy way, O Lord, teach me Thy way!
Thy guiding grace afford, teach me Thy way!
Help me to walk aright, more by faith, less by sight;
Lead me with heav'nly light, teach me Thy way!
When I am sad at heart, teach me Thy way!
When earthly joys depart, teach me Thy way!
In hours of loneliness, in times of dire distress,
In failure or success, teach me Thy way!
When doubts and fears arise, teach me Thy way!
When storms o'erspread the skies, teach me Thy way!
Shine thro' the cloud and rain, thro' sorrow, toil
    and pain;
Make Thou my pathway plain, teach me Thy way!

—B. Mansell Ramsey

October 3

God of rest and rejuvenation, guide me to find ways to let your nurturing reach me. I need to be healthy and well-rested in order to provide, lead, and inspire. Burning the candle at both ends all the time is hardly an example I'm proud of.

If I'm loving others the way I'm loving myself, we're all in trouble. May God awaken me to my life so I can help my kids be awake to theirs.

October 4

Children are a blessing and a gift from the Lord.

Psalm 127:3 CEV

Lord, with the children all in school, how quiet the house is! It is almost eerie not to hear the high-pitched squeals and laughter, the screams and the cries.

Is this the way it will be when they all grow up and move out of the house? Will sadness and loneliness invade our home? I am lonely for my children already, Lord.

Will you comfort me when they are gone, and send other gifts to take their places, like mates for my children, good marriages, the establishment of homes where you will dwell, and, maybe someday, grandchildren?

For now I'll be content with the sounds of children filling up the house once more. I will not complain, and I will enjoy these gifts as long as I can. They will be gone too soon.

October 5

I f my lips could sing as many songs as there
are waves in the sea:
if my tongue could sing as many hymns as there are
ocean billows:
if my mouth filled the whole firmament with praise:
if my face shone like the sun and moon together:
if my hands were to hover in the sky like powerful
eagles and my feet ran across mountains as swiftly as
the deer;
all that would not be enough to pay you fitting tribute,
O Lord my God.

—Jewish Prayer

*I am certain that God will bless me,
but I don't need to know how.
When we think we know exactly how
the one who made us is going to take care of us,
we're apt to ignore the angel messengers
sent us along the way.*

—Madeleine L'Engle, *Glimpses of Grace*

October 6

*Day by day, as they spent much time together in the temple,
they broke bread at home and ate their food with glad and generous
hearts, praising God and having the goodwill of all the people.*

Acts 2:46–47

When we are missing an important ingredient in the recipe, we sometimes substitute something that will work for the ideal. Remind us, O Lord, that when it comes to nourishing our family ties, there is no substitute for genuine sharing and caring.

*The fare, while important,
doesn't have to be gourmet to bring
joy into the hearts about our tables.
Rather, generous portions of laughter and
caring nourish our table guests by exposing
them to love and assuring them of
their special places in our lives.*

October 7

Be still, and know that I am God! I am exalted among the nations, I am exalted in the earth.

Psalm 46:10

God, I am scurrying around like a chicken with its head cut off, making a huge mess everywhere I go. Why, God, when I know I do better and work more efficiently when I wait quietly and listen for your guidance, do I rush about—driven by time rather than by you?

Help me, God, to slow down, to be silent, so I can hear you and do your will, not mine.

Remember: Silent is an anagram of Listen.

October 8

Now we have received not the spirit of the world, but the Spirit that is from God, so that we may understand the gifts bestowed on us by God.

1 Corinthians 2:12

Help me take stock of your gifts to me, Lord. I'm good at things that appear to be so insignificant. Chances are you can use any one of them, no matter how simple it appears, to help others. Remind me that it's not what I do but my doing that ultimately matters.

Does God ask us to do what is beneath us?
This question will never trouble us again if we consider
the Lord of heaven taking a towel and washing feet.

—Elisabeth Elliot, *Discipline—The Glad Surrender*

October 9

In quietness and in confidence shall be your strength.

Isaiah 30:15 KJV

Lord, I try so hard to be a good mother that I'm sure I do too much for my family. Being all things to all people only leaves me tired and resentful, and that is not good for any of us.

You know what is best for my children, Lord. Help me to hold back so I don't do those things they can do for themselves. Help me to build in my youngsters a sense of confidence. Make them reliable rather than overdependent, strong rather than weak.

You are our strength and our song, O God. May we sing your words loud and clear.

*The more confident your children become,
the less hostile they will be.
Independence is power.*

October 10

Lord, you have been our dwelling place in all generations.

Psalm 90:1

*T*hank you, loving God, for my mother with whom I share a connection to the children. For it was her loving care and ceaseless attention that empowered me to mother. I am humbled by her stead-fastness. I am a much-blessed daughter.

There is a special place in our hearts carved out just for memories.

—Marianne Richmond,
The Gift of a Memory

October 11

Rejoice always, pray without ceasing, give thanks in all circumstances.

1 Thessalonians 5:16–18

In all things, give thanks. In the good days of laughter and joy, give thanks.

In the bad days of struggle and strife, give thanks.

In the brightest moments and the darkest hours, give thanks.

In the flow of blessings and the apparent lack of goodness, give thanks.

In the face of fortune and misfortune, give thanks.

In the presence of pleasure and pain, give thanks.

In all things, give thanks.

For lessons and blessings are found not just in the light, but in the darkness.

Even in the face of struggles and difficulties,
there is a higher order of goodness at work in our lives.
We may not be able to physically detect it at all times,
but our faith knows the truth, and the truth sets us free.

Lord,
 Keep my parents in your love.
Lord,
bless them and keep them.
Lord,
please let me have money and strength
and keep my parents for many more years
so that I can take care of them.

—A Young Ghanaian Christian

How marvelous to be connected to an extended family!
I am so grateful to those who have brought us to who
we are today. I am honored to be part of this family.

October 13

By wisdom a house is built, and by understanding it is established; by knowledge the rooms are filled with all precious and pleasant riches.

Proverbs 24:3–4

Bless our homes, dear God, that we cherish the daily bread before there is none, discover each other before we leave on our separate ways, and enjoy each other for what we are, while we have time to do so.

—A Prayer from Hawaii (adapted)

We are living in times when mouths are open, tongues are flapping, and we are quick to talk, giving sound bites of advice rather than truly listening to others. The result is that we share neither wisdom nor understanding, and those we treasure the most are left feeling alone and unheard.

October 14

I always want to be a dreamer, O God, to feel the stir and the yearning to see my vision become reality. There are those who would say dreamers are free-floaters. When I dream I feel connected to you and to your creation, bound by purpose and a sense of call. Nourish my dreams and my striving to make them real.

Hold fast to dreams
For if dreams die
Life is a broken-winged bird
That cannot fly.
Hold fast to dreams
For when dreams go
Life is a barren field
Frozen with snow.

—Langston Hughes

October 15

Abide in me as I abide in you. Just as the branch cannot bear fruit by itself unless it abides in the vine, neither can you unless you abide in me. I am the vine, you are the branches. Those who abide in me and I in them bear much fruit.

John 15:4–5

Lord, I do not say, "Be with me," for of course you are! . . . I praise you for your faithfulness and mercies that you offer new every morning. Thank you for showing me that I do not have to generate answers—I simply must stay plugged into you, the true vine.

Increase my vision, Lord. May I not be content with the status quo, but may I freely share with others what you have given me. Lord, give me grace to learn the joys of obedience. And may I rehearse your amazing goodness continually. Amen.

—Nancie Carmichael, *Desperate for God*

Take my life and let it be
Consecrated, Lord, to Thee;
Take my hands and let them move
At the impulse of Thy love,
At the impulse of Thy love.
Take my feet and let them be
Swift and beautiful for Thee;
Take my voice and let me sing
Always, only, for my King,
Always, only, for my King.
Take my silver and my gold,
Not a mite would I withhold;
Take my moments and my days,
Let them flow in ceaseless praise,
Let them flow in ceaseless praise.
Take my will and make it Thine,
It shall be no longer mine;
Take my heart, it is Thine own,
It shall be Thy royal throne,
It shall be Thy royal throne.

—Frances R. Havergal

October 17

They will come and shout for joy . . .
they will rejoice in the bounty of the Lord.

Jeremiah 31:12 NIV

Despite tiredness and worry, I have moments of sheer, cartwheeling, rainbow-dancing pride and joy. I hope there are times when you say that of me. Maybe today, as I join my kids to play in the leaves, make snow angels, pack a picnic, learn the latest dance move, share pizza, or just celebrate being together. Take our hands, and jump with us for joy!

Parenthood should be a twenty-year adventure,
not a twenty-year sentence.

—Dr. Henry Brandt and Phil Landrum, *I Want to Enjoy my Children*

October 18

For mortals it is impossible, but for God all things are possible.

Matthew 19:26

So often we wallow in our children's problems rather than exult in their strengths and possibilities. So often we dwell on the things that seem impossible rather than on the things that are possible. So often we are depressed by what remains to be done and forget to be thankful for all that has been done. Forgive us God.

—Marian Wright Edelman, *Guide My Feet*

October 19

*I will try to walk a blameless path, but how I need your help,
especially in my own home, where I long to act as I should.*

Psalm 101:2 LB

Grant that we may realize that it is the little
things that create differences, that in the big
things of life we are at one. And may we strive to touch
and to know the great, common heart of us all, and,
Oh Lord God, let us forget not to be kind!

—Mary Stewart

*Time-outs are equally good for cranky adults as for
disobedient children, sending us to a quiet place to
think about our actions, attitudes, and moods.
And in that quiet moment, an intervening God
comes to hold and inspire us to better days ahead.*

October 20

I came so that everyone would have life, and have it in its fullest.

John 10:10 CEV

Giver of life and all good gifts:
   Grant us also wisdom to use
only what we need;
Courage to trust our bounty;
Imagination to preserve our resources;
Determination to deny frivolous excess;
And inspiration to sustain through temptation.

—Patricia Winters

God will give you knowledge and wisdom.
From him you will receive understanding
for God has been storing up wisdom for you
because you have sought him above all else.

—Marilyn Willett Heavilin, *Becoming a Woman of Honor*

October 21

Let us therefore approach the throne of grace with boldness, so that we may receive mercy and find grace to help in time of need.

Hebrews 4:16

Thou hast promised to receive us,
Poor and sinful though we be;
Thou hast mercy to relieve us,
Grace to cleanse, and pow'r to free:
Blessed Jesus, blessed Jesus,
Early let us turn to thee;
Blessed Jesus, blessed Jesus,
Early let us turn to thee.

Early let us seek thy favor;
Early let us do thy will;
Blessed Lord and only Savior
With thy love our bosoms fill:
Blessed Jesus, blessed Jesus,
Thou hast loved us, love us still;
Blessed Jesus, blessed Jesus,
Thou hast loved us, love us still.

—Dorothy Thrupp, "Savior, Like a Shepherd Lead Us"

October 22

God is truly good . . . especially to everyone with a pure heart.

Psalm 73:1 CEV

ord, may everything we do begin with your inspiration and continue with your help so that all our prayers and works may begin in you and by you be happily ended.

—Gertrud Mueller Nelson and Christopher Witt, *Pocket Prayers*

The very word God *suggests care, kindness, goodness; and the idea of God in his infinity is infinite care, infinite kindness, infinite goodness. We give God the name of good: it is only by shortening it that it becomes God.*

—Henry Ward Beecher

October 23

Be careful then how you live, not as unwise people but as wise, making the most of the time.

Ephesians 5:15–16

How easily, O God of eternity, for us to assume our time is like the grains of sand on an ocean beach—vast and endless. Remind us that each of our lives is limited like the sand in the hour-glass. May what we do with that sand—play in it, work in it, build our relationships, whatever—be wise use of this precious gift of living.

Our goal for living should not be to save time but to savor it.

October 24

*The Lord is good, a stronghold in a day of trouble;
he protects those who take refuge in him.*

Nahum 1:7

Almighty God, the world is a fearsome place where violence is glorified, disease is rampant, and young children are victimized daily. I am afraid for my family, but you are our refuge and strength, and we seek protection under the shadow of your wings (Psalm 57:1).

Continue to guard my loved ones, Lord: my husband, my children, and all others so dear to me. Preserve them from harm, guard them from the pain of sorrow and suffering, and bless them with good health.

In times of trouble, arm us for the battle and guide us safely through it. Our confidence is with you.

October 25

Unless the Lord builds the house, its builders labor in vain.

Psalm 127:1 NIV

*S*it with me, God of broken dreams, in the debris of my family. Toddler tantrums, teen rebellion, young-adult resistance. They topple me like a tornado through town even in this time of peacemaking. I'm tempted to finish the destruction with harsh words, yet how can I reject or give up on a child loved by you no matter how much upheaval they cause? Keep me calm.

October 26

Blessed are those who have not seen and yet have come to believe.

John 20:29

We sit around the table, my family and I, and celebrate the blessings God has given us. Blessings of loved ones, of good food, and of the shared bounty of the earth. Blessings of a warm, happy home filled with laughter and joy. Blessings of times spent together, of achievements and successes. Blessings of lessons we've learned, of silver linings surrounding every dark cloud, and of rainbows following every dreary shower. But mostly we celebrate our faith: in each other and in God. Faith is the foundation of our strength, the bedrock of our joy.

October 27

Happy are those who trust in the Lord.

Proverbs 16:20

Come unto me, ye weary,
And I will give you rest.
O blessed voice of Jesus,
Which comes to hearts opprest;
It tells of benediction,
Of pardon, grace and peace,
Of joy that hath no ending,
Of love which cannot cease.
Come unto Me, ye wanderers,
And I will give you light,
O loving voice of Jesus,
Which comes to cheer the night.
Our hearts were fill'd with sadness
And we had lost our way,
But He has brought us gladness
And songs at break of day.

—*The Book of Common Prayer*

October 28

*Jesus went back to Nazareth, where he had been brought up,
and as usual he went to the meeting place on the Sabbath.
When he stood up to read from the Scriptures, he was given
the book of Isaiah the prophet. He opened it and read.*

Luke 4:16–17 CEV

Your son, Jesus, was a reader, Lord. He read from your own books, the Holy Scriptures. Books can change us. They can transport us to other places and other times and can share the wisdom of the ages.

I love books and reading and want my children to treasure them, too. Thank you, Lord, for good books, especially the Bible, that can feed our children's minds and imaginations and can show us the wonder of life in your world.

*Books are one of life's greatest treasures.
They give us minds to enter, lives to live,
and conversations with the past.*

October 29

We are the children of God.

Romans 8:16 KJV

Lord, I suppose in every family there is a child whose self-esteem suffers by comparison with siblings. Let me be sensitive to the subtle messages my children are receiving within the family circle, regarding their self-worth.

Help me to show my confidence in each child and to remind them all that they matter to our family. They also matter to you, Lord, for you are the God who cares for and values each of your children.

Give my young ones the assurance that comes with knowing they are the children of the King.

To know we are the children of the King
brings all the self-esteem we need.

October 30

Jesus said to him, "If you are able!—All things can be done for the one who believes." Immediately the father of the child cried out, "I believe; help my unbelief!"

Mark 9:23–24

Sometimes my doubts are so strong and so bothersome. Give me courage to express my doubts to you, O God, knowing that they are necessary moments through which I can pass on my way to true contentment in you.

Accept doubts that come about mothering, about children, about the future—whatever— for they are magnifying glasses that clarify thoughts, beliefs, and dreams and strengthen resolve that in God's hands becomes more than enough.

October 31

If you love your children, you will correct them.

Proverbs 13:24 NCV

e're making costumes this year, Lord, instead of buying prepackaged identities. I'm so proud of my children. Help me guide them toward independence, not sheeplike conformity. Help me to respect their need to belong to their world, while finding a way to link it to mine.

How tricky it can be to help the children fit into their world without becoming of the world. God can gently guide us as we guide their choices into what is safe and okay to "follow" and what is not.

My Prayer Life

_____

_____

_____

_____

_____

_____

_____

_____

_____

_____

_____

November 1

For you have delivered my soul from death, and my feet from falling,
so that I may walk before God in the light of life.

Psalm 56:13

In this day of bigger is best, Lord, we wonder
what difference our little lights can make.
Remind us of the laser: so tiny, yet when focused, has
incredible power. This little light of
mine, O Lord, give it such focus.

If there is light in the soul,
there will be beauty in the person.
If there is beauty in the person,
there will be harmony in the home.
If there is harmony in the home,
there will be order in the nation.
If there is order in the nation,
there will be peace in the world.

—Chinese Proverb

November 2

Take my instruction instead of silver, and knowledge rather than choice gold; for wisdom is better than jewels, and all that you may desire cannot compare with her.

Proverbs 8:10–11

Heavenly Father, the writer of Proverbs values knowledge and education, and so do I. Please enable me to impart my love of learning to my children so they can meet the challenges of the schoolroom with confidence and a sense of adventure.

Give me the insight to know when to help them with schoolwork and when to back off. Show me how to strike a balance between pressing for higher achievement and accepting what is accomplished. Above all, make me an encourager, not a hindrance to the learning process.

Lord, you are the great teacher. Teach me to inspire my children to reach their highest potentials and use their education to glorify you.

A mother may be the most important book her child will ever read.

November 3

I will give thanks to the Lord with my whole heart;
I will tell of all your wonderful deeds.

Psalm 9:1

Lord, behold our family here assembled. We thank you for this place in which we dwell, for the love that unites us, for the peace accorded us this day, for the hope with which we expect the morrow; for the health, the work, the food and the bright skies that make our lives delightful; for our friends in all parts of the earth. Amen.

—Robert Louis Stevenson

November 4

Lord, through all the generations, you have been our home!

Psalm 90:1 LB

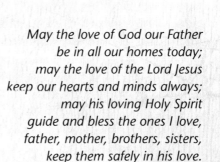

hat transforms ordinary events into lifelong traditions? What makes paper chains into holy relics and gluey, lopsided homemade gifts into icons? Love! Inspire me to show my kids the divine love, the holiness, in the ordinary.

May the love of God our Father
be in all our homes today;
may the love of the Lord Jesus
keep our hearts and minds always;
may his loving Holy Spirit
guide and bless the ones I love,
father, mother, brothers, sisters,
keep them safely in his love.

—*Infant Prayers*

November 5

Trust in the Lord with all your heart, and do not rely on your own insight. In all your ways acknowledge him, and he will make straight your paths.

Proverbs 3:5–6

Dear Lord, I give each member of my family to you. I am sure you love them with a perfect love. Since you have greater knowledge of their needs, I know I can trust you to watch over them. Whatever happens, I acknowledge that you are sovereign, and you are in control.

—Fran Caffey Sandin, *See You Later, Jeffrey*

November 6

Pleasant words are like a honeycomb,
sweetness to the soul and health to the body.

Proverbs 16:24

Gentle Lord, for the first time I listened to myself as I frantically got the family ready for school. In my frustration, I barked out orders and hurled angry words in every direction. No wonder the children are in a grumpy mood. I know it's time I changed my tune.

Grant me more patience, Lord, and teach me how to guard my tongue. Make my words soothing and sweet like the honeycomb, so my children can arrive at school in a calmer, happier frame of mind. Teach me the lesson, Lord, that pleasant words get better results.

November 7

You will be secure, because there is hope;
and you will look about you and take your rest in safety.

Job 11:18 NIV

Dear God, be good to me;
   The sea is so wide,
And my boat is so small.

—Breton Fishermen's Prayer

It's easy to forget that children have problems
too—like fitting in, measuring up, looking OK.
God never turns away from even the smallest
concern, a lesson to teach daily.

November 8

I have set my bow in the clouds.

Refocus me, God of love, to embrace and enjoy this child growing so quickly into independence. When growth pains come, send me a rainbow of friends' support, vision, and patience to enjoy, although it's sure to rain again. Help me accept storm and sun as the balance of nature, of life.

*The thread of our life would be dark,
heaven knows, if it were not with
friendship and love intertwined.*

—Sir Thomas More, *Friendship Is a Special Gift*

November 9

But God is my helper. He is a friend of mine!

Psalm 54:4 LB

Touch and calm my turbulent emotions, God of the still waters. Whisper words to the listening ears of my soul. In hearing your voice, give me assurance beyond a shadow of a doubt that you are my companion in life, eternally.

O God, you are my comforter,
my stick-beside-me friend.
How wonderful you are!
There, there I seem to hear you say.
Be still now, and just remember
that I'm your God.

—Elspeth Campbell Murphy, *Sometimes I Have to Cry*

November 10

Therefore be imitators of
God, as beloved children,
and live in love, as Christ loved us.

Ephesians 5:1–2

A family's love is as sure as the taste of an orange,
as certain as the flow of water toward the sea,
as familiar as the fragrance of a rose
even after the bloom has faded,
and as steadfast as the warmth of the sun.

Lord, how is it that when I lift my eyes to thee
    so often all I see is that splat of oatmeal on the
kitchen ceiling and a new crack in the paint?
I want to do glorious deeds—
but I have to iron shirts
And bake cupcakes for the Brownie meeting.
I want to be a saint—one of the architects of the
    kingdom—
but you know better than I do that I'm considerably
    less than a saint.

*And yet somehow the most honest meditation I have known
has happened over an ironing board. A most honest sort of
love can be stirred into a batch of cupcakes.*

—Jo Carr and Imogene Sorley

November 12

We are the clay, and you are our potter; we are all the work of your hand.

Isaiah 64:8

Have thine
own way,
  Lord!
Have thine own way!
Thou art the potter,
I am the clay!
Mold me and make me
After thy will,
While I am waiting,
Yielded and still.

Have thine own way,
  Lord!
Have thine own way!
Search me and try me,
Master, today!
Whiter than snow, Lord,
Wash me just now,
As in thy presence
Humbly I bow.

Have thine own way,
  Lord!
Have thine own way!
Wounded and weary,
Help me, I pray!
Power, all power,
Surely is thine!
Touch me and heal me,
Savior divine.

Have thine own way,
  Lord!
Have thine own way!
Hold o'er my being
Absolute sway!
Fill with thy Spirit
Till all shall be
Christ only always,
Living in me.
Amen.

—Adelaide A. Pollard

November 13

Sometimes, God, I get too persnickety and alarmingly tidy. I suppose I think it's a way I can control my life. When that happens, shake me up like a snow globe so I can be real. Truly, messily, and welcomingly real.

The beauty of a home is harmony,
the security of a house is loyalty,
the joy of a house is love,
the rule of a house is service,
the comfort of a house is in contented spirits.
The real home is a place of real living.

—James L. Christensen, *New Ways to Worship*

November 14

The eye is the lamp of the body. So, if your eye is healthy,
your whole body will be full of light.

Matthew 6:22

Open my eyes that I may see
    Glimpses of truth thou sendest me;
Place in my hands the wonderful key
That shall unclasp, and set me free:
Silently now I wait for thee,
Ready, my God, thy will to see;
Open my eyes, illumine me, Spirit divine!

Open my ears that I may hear
Voices of truth thou sendest clear;
And while the wavenotes fall on my ear,
Ev'rything false will disappear:
Silently now I wait for thee,
Ready my God, thy will to see;
Open my heart illumine me, Spirit divine!

—Clara H. Scott

Everything you have endured, suffered,
or experienced can have eternal value
if you will view it from God's perspective.

—Kay Arthur, *Lord, Heal My Hurts*

November 15

Fools think their own way is right, but the wise listen to advice.

Proverbs 12:15

Two ears, one mouth? Perhaps a hint, subtle or not, about what is more important in life, Great God. Make me at least as ready to listen as I am to talk. Give me patience to listen to the concerns, the hopes, the dreams of these important people called family, for that is how we connect. There are times to talk and times to listen. Please help me to know the difference.

November 16

Your love means more than life to me, and I praise you.

Psalm 63:3 CEV

ord, why is it that we mothers feel embarrassed when our youngsters misbehave in public? They are just being children, yet our cheeks burn with shame when they are less than perfect. Then, to cover our embarrassment, we treat them unfairly or embarrass them.

Forgive me when I react to my children in a less-than-loving way, Father. You never withhold your love from me. Grant me the wisdom and understanding to deal with problems before they get out of hand; to avoid the anger that clouds my good judgment.

Childhood passes so quickly. I don't want to spend it scolding and reprimanding. Show me how to deal with my children in loving kindness, as you do, and to let them know how much they mean to me.

*The art of gentle persuasion
is a mother's most potent weapon.*

November 17

Let your steadfast love, O Lord, be upon us, even as we hope in you.

Psalm 33:22

Trying to find relief on "those days," it's so easy to forget that the world's way of TV, computer games, shopping, snacking, and other guilty pleasures is no substitute for God's companionship and guidance.

God of your goodness give me yourself,
for you are sufficient for me.
I cannot properly ask anything less,
to be worthy of you. If I were to ask less,
I should always be in want. In you alone do I have all.

—Julian of Norwich

November 18

Send out your bread upon the waters,
for after many days you will get it back.

Ecclesiastes 11:1

A mother's prayer is a powerful force because it is so close to the heart of a creating God. They have often prayed a wayward husband into heaven or a prodigal child back to virtue. Their loving concern makes the children sense that the home is like a church pointing in the direction of heaven, where our real home and citizenship truly lie.

Dear Lord, make every mother see how her vocation is a priestly one: to give and nourish life, to pray for and stimulate God-life in her children and others, to be a creative force in the world.

—*The Pilgrim's Prayer Book*

She was good as she was fair,
None—none on earth above her!
As pure in thought as angels are:
To know her was to love her.

—Samuel Rogers

November 19

For you were called to freedom, brothers and sisters; only do not use your freedom as an opportunity for self-indulgence, but through love become slaves to one another.

Galatians 5:13

From infancy, it's hard not to choose for your child. It's a riddle, O God, why you give us freedom to choose. Didn't you know it could break a mother's heart? Comfort me as I cope with a choice not mine; forgive any role I had in it. Keep me from saying, "I told you so."

Though parents may relate differently to a child, . . . each can teach the child that she is valuable and worthwhile, able and capable, and supply her with the materials and emotional encouragement for learning and developing into the person God made her able to be.

—C. Sybil Waldrop, *Guiding Your Child Toward God*

November 20

Let your hope make you glad. Be patient in time of trouble and never stop praying.

Romans 12:12 CEV

Loving Father, the source of all life, and provider for all mankind: Remind us of the privilege and responsibility we have as families. We have no homes without your presence; and no family without your fatherhood. Rebuild our homes to be a source of life and love, with Christ Jesus being our chief cornerstone; in whose name we pray. Amen.

—Heth H. Corl, *Continuity in Contemporary Worship*

Nothing about God's children is too trivial or ordinary, too overwhelming or dreadful to be overlooked. God's ear is as close as a bent knee, a bowed head, or clasped hands. We simply need to plug ourselves into God's nurturing care.

November 21

Dear God, for another day, for another minute, for another chance to live and serve you, I am grateful. Please keep me free from fear of the future, from anxiety about tomorrow, from bitterness towards anyone, from cowardice in the face of danger, from laziness in my daily work, from failure before opportunity, from weakness when your power is at hand. But fill me with love that knows no bounds, with sympathy that reaches all, with courage that cannot be shaken, with faith strong enough for the darkness, with strength sufficient for my tasks. Be with me for another day, and use me as you will. Amen.

—*The Pilgrim's Prayer Book*

For it is only the finite that has wrought and suffered; the infinite lies stretched in smiling repose.

—Ralph Waldo Emerson

November 22

Many, O Lord my God, are the wonders you have done.

Psalm 40:5 NIV

We're making decorations from pipe cleaners, clay, and crayons, O God, and talking about all we have to be thankful for. You have blessed us richly. We hope you enjoy the pictures the children are drawing of our bounty, for in their simplicity, they capture the essence of our gratitude.

Reflect on your present blessings,
of which every man has many;
not on your past misfortunes,
of which all men have some.

—Charles Dickens

November 23

Enter his gates with thanksgiving, and his courts with praise.
Give thanks to him, bless his name.

Psalm 100:4

Dear God,

You have blessed me with a loving, caring husband; wonderful kids; a beautiful home; friends that I
can depend on; and work that I love to do. We are all
healthy, and for that I give thanks. We are all happy,
and for that I give thanks. We are all blessed, but no
one more so than me. You have given me the gift
of motherhood and of a family that means so
much to me, and I will forever
be grateful.

Take the time to slow down and count your
blessings. Gratitude is magnetic. When
you focus on the good in your life, it
tends to attract even more.

November 24

Let your work be manifest to your servants, and your glorious power to their children. Let the favor of the Lord our God be upon us.

Psalm 90:16–17

Blessed are you, O God, for the gift of life you have bestowed upon your children. We thank you for the mothers of this world who nurture their children to adulthood with patience, love, and understanding. We thank you for the comfort they give in times of pain and sorrow, for the hope they bring through their sustaining faith, and for the encouragement they offer as they seek new life for their beloved children.

—Vienna Cobb Anderson

*When we give thanks and praise to someone,
we honor the presence of God in that person.
Our gratitude for the people we love
is our acknowledgment of the
Holy Spirit's working through them.*

November 25

Precious Lord, fostering kindness in children isn't easy because they are so centered on their own wants and needs. But Lord, I praise you for signs of kindness I have seen in my children. As they grow, I see more evidence of their reaching out to others, and I am thankful.

Your Word has said we are to be imitators of you, to live in love, to be forgiving and tenderhearted. I have tried to be kind and loving in all circumstances, but I have not always succeeded. Yet in your tender mercy, you have allowed some of your goodness to shine through to my children.

Continue to develop in their hearts a compassion for the poor, the ill, the unfortunate, the outcast, so each day they may grow more like you.

To show kindness is to scatter joy
and strength to those who need it most.

November 26

Even youths will faint and be weary, and the young will fall exhausted.

Isaiah 40:30

There is in your grace, God of second chances, insufficient evidence to prove my latest setback is a failure. Even if it is, with you, failure is never final but an opportunity to learn and grow. When I goof, as I am prone to do, help me from doubling the problem by failing to take advantage of your redemption.

Why am I so contrary? I wonder and worry. Perhaps it is tiredness, frustration, pressure, but too often I lose my cool and then the children do likewise until we have a mess and muddle. I'm so grateful that God can help repair it.

November 27

For the Lord God is a sun and shield; he bestows favor and honor.
No good thing does the Lord withhold from those who walk uprightly.

Psalm 84:11

Sun of our life, thy quickening ray
    Shed on our path the glow of day;
Star of our hope, thy softened light
Cheers the long watches of the night.

Our midnight is thy smile withdrawn;
Our noontide is thy gracious dawn;
Our rainbow arch thy mercy's sign;
All, save the clouds of sin, are thine!

Lord of all life, below, above,
Whose light is truth, whose warmth is love,
Before thy ever-blazing throne
We ask no lustre of our own.

Grant us thy truth to make us free,
And kindling hearts that burn for thee,
Till all thy living altars claim
One holy light, one heavenly flame!

—Oliver Wendell Holmes, "A Sun-day Hymn"

November 28

I am with you always.

Matthew 28:20

As I gently teach, lead, and guide from this nest of family, O God, may I be a resource and a companion, not a know-it-all busybody. Guide me to assure my kids, as you do me, then ease into the background. They'll know where to find me.

*May there always be work
for your hands to do.
May your purse always hold
a coin or two.
May the sun always shine
upon your window pane.
May a rainbow be certain
to follow each rain.
May the hand of a friend
always be near to you and
May God fill your heart
with gladness to cheer you.*

—Irish Blessing

November 29

I now realize how true it is that God does not show favoritism.

Acts 10:34 NIV

Lord, I love all of my children. Each is unique and precious to me. I want them to be assured that I could not choose one over the other and that even though my actions may be perceived as partiality, I do not play favorites.

Playing favorites can be destructive. Joseph's brothers were torn apart by their father's partiality to him. King Saul was driven mad by the favoritism the public showed David.

You treat all people alike, Lord. We are all your children. Please help me to do the same, and guard me from even the appearance of favoritism. Thank you for making each one of us feel like your favorite.

All of my children are God's favorites—
and mine.

November 30

I say of the holy people who are in the land,
"They are the noble ones in whom is all my delight."

Psalm 16:3 NIV

We are big on heroes, God. Every area of our lives has a favorite except perhaps the most important: our faith. An Aquinas or Augustine can't hold a candle to the Hollywood celebrities of our day. How sad we willingly settle for superficiality rather than substance. Help us desire to be grounded as well as entertained.

Seek a quiet corner to give thanks for the saints whose day this really is. Remember those pillars of faith upon whose shoulders we stand. A marvelous opportunity—in the midst of candy and costumes—to introduce them to the children.

My Prayer Life

December 1

So often, Patient One, we become stifled, leading to boredom and whining when circumstances are not as we would have them. What power there is in seeing things not as they are but as they might be, O God, as the children—and I—learn invaluable truths as close as our own backyard!

Moms know what to do with hamburger, fabric scraps, and winter: Make meatloaf, quilts, and windowsill gardens, showing our children how to live "as if." As if useless can become useful, as if seemingly dead can live, as if spring will come, God's renewing love is scattered around like posies in a garden of grace.

December 2

Be filled with the Spirit, as you sing psalms and hymns and spiritual songs, . . . singing and making melody to the Lord in your hearts.

Ephesians 5:18–19

In my attempts to "get it right" as I order my life and the lives of those in my family, remind me, O Creator God, to look around and see how you have brought order to our world. Such balance, such harmony, such stability. May I find the faith to trust you like a bird trusts the winds that allow it to soar.

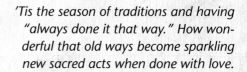

'Tis the season of traditions and having "always done it that way." How wonderful that old ways become sparkling new sacred acts when done with love.

December 3

*Jesus said to them again, "Peace be with you. As the Father has sent me,
so I send you." When he had said this, he breathed on them
and said to them, "Receive the Holy Spirit."*

John 20:21–22

Breathe on me, Breath of God,
Fill me with life anew,
That I may love what Thou dost love,
And do what Thou wouldst do.
Breathe on me, Breath of God,
Until my heart is pure,
Until with Thee I will Thy will,
To do and to endure.
Breathe on me, Breath of God,
Till I am wholly Thine,
Till all this earthly part of me
Glows with Thy fire divine.
Breathe on me, Breath of God,
So shall I never die,
But live with Thee the perfect life
Of Thine eternity.
Amen.

—Edwin Hatch

December 4

But ask in faith, never doubting, for the one who doubts
is like a wave of the sea, driven and tossed by the wind.

James 1:6

O God by whom the meek are guided in judgment, and light riseth up in the darkness for
the godly; grant us, in all our doubts and uncertainties,
the grace to ask what thou wouldst have us do; that the
Spirit of Wisdom may save us from all false choices and
that in thy light we may see light, and in thy straight
path may not stumble; through Jesus Christ our Lord.

—William Bright

How tempting to wonder
"Am I doing okay?"
and then look around and
think others are doing better—
in abilities, wisdom, faith.
May God take these doubts
and do something with them
so as not to stay stuck in them!

December 5

God, instill in my children the heart of an adventurer off to explore every corner of your marvelous creation and to find their place in it. Thank you for blessing the quest and relieving my anxiety by promising to be a part of their journey step by step.

Explore the earth as you now find it.
Solve new mysteries; find the stone.
Crawl to where the sphere turns firmament.
Isolate to know for certain you are not alone.
Touch the wedding of the waters:
See the elements combine.
Read the wordless book of nature
Where the spirit's clearly writ.
Make the modern magic thine.
Go, my child, into the world.
Find yourself in knowing it.

—Maureen Tolman Flannery

December 6

Pursue peace with everyone,
and the holiness without which no one will see the Lord.

Hebrews 12:14

Give me the tools for building peace, O God,
when tempers flare—inside and outside these
four walls. In your wisdom I daily try to impart, needed
tools include a kind heart and faith that measures each
tiny rebuilt bridge a triumph.

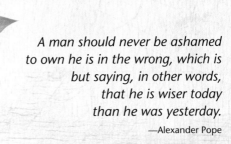

A man should never be ashamed
to own he is in the wrong, which is
but saying, in other words,
that he is wiser today
than he was yesterday.

—Alexander Pope

December 7

Even though I walk through the darkest valley, I fear no evil;
for you are with me.

December 7

Even though I walk through the darkest valley, I fear no evil;
for you are with me.

Psalm 23:4

God help our children seek and find
Your words and ways, trustworthy
friends and loving companions to share
their days. Guard them against the
poisonous arrows of malice and violence
and drugs and hate and arrogance . . . on
their journeys to adulthood.

—Marian Wright Edelman, *Guide My Feet*

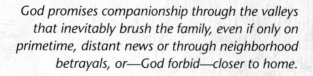

God promises companionship through the valleys
that inevitably brush the family, even if only on
primetime, distant news or through neighborhood
betrayals, or—God forbid—closer to home.

December 8

Rejoice greatly, O daughter Zion!... Lo, your king comes to you... and he shall command peace to the nations.

Zechariah 9:9–10

At Advent we should try the key to our heart's door. It may have gathered rust. If so, this is the time to oil it, in order that the heart's door may open more easily when the Lord Jesus wants to enter at Christmas time.

Lord, oil the hinges of our hearts' doors that they may swing gently and easily to welcome your coming.

—Mary Batchelor

*Shopping, wrapping, traveling, cooking.
So much to do this season as we hurry
toward the manger, answering God's call
as did those folk so long ago, to go,
believe, and do. Practice the notes of the carol,
for soon it will be time to sing out,
"Gloria!" at what we'll see and hear.*

December 9

The Lord, my God, lights up my darkness.

Psalm 18:28

O God, when all the world looks gray and dirt
shows everywhere and nothing is as it should be,
I wonder if you really are.

O God, help me when I feel like this: Help me to
remember the days when you were near and I knew it.
Even when you seem far away, help me never to turn
my back on you. Set me on the path to you and help me
hold fast through the night, until I find your light once
more.

—Avery Brooke, *Plain Prayers for a Complicated World*

*Expect periods of hardship to occur,
and don't be dismayed when they arrive.
"Lean into the pain" when your time
to suffer comes around, knowing that God
will use the difficulty for his purposes—
and indeed, for our own good.*

—Dr. James Dobson, *When God Doesn't Make Sense*

December 10

Lord of all creation, my heart soars as I think of this child growing and moving within me. Like Mary, I sing your praises, O God. My spirit rejoices and spills over in thankfulness for this gift, this miracle that you have given us.

Lord, you have given me the privilege to be a part of your creation. I feel blessed among women. Please make me a fit vessel for my children. Make me worthy of your trust in me, and help me to become the kind of parent you want me to be.

December 11

Whenever you face trials of any kind, consider it nothing but joy,
because you know that the testing of your faith produces endurance…
so that you may be mature and complete, lacking in nothing.

James 1:2–4

Lord, motherhood is full of trials that have tested my faith. And, yes, I have developed perseverance and maturity. But sometimes I still need James' reminder to "consider it nothing but joy."

In the midst of these trials, I am often ready to give up, to weep and wail over my misfortune; but you are there, Lord, to comfort me. You come to me with your healing touch to wipe away my sorrow.

With your help, Father, I have so far managed to survive each trial intact, with the joy far outweighing the pain. As I hug each of my children and hold them tight, I thank you, Lord.

As any airline passenger knows,
the sun is still shining on the other side of that cloud.

December 12

Be renewed in the spirit of your minds.

I get discouraged, O God, my comforter and guide, and feel overwhelmed, which makes me even more discouraged. Lead me beyond negative thoughts and useless circles of worry to a renewed frame of mind. Work your miracle of transformation in me.

Rule your mind, which, if it is not your servant, is your master.

—Horace

December 13

Let us continually offer a sacrifice of praise to God.

Hebrews 13:15

Lord, I've learned how to pray in strange but necessary places: in car pools, while cooking dinner, at the dentist, between loads of laundry, waiting in the checkout line. I've discovered that it's not how long I pray that matters but rather the very act of attempting to make a connection with you.

Hope is the thing with feathers—
That perches in the soul—
And sings the tune without the words—
And never stops—at all.

—Emily Dickinson

December 14

Set an example for other followers by what you say and do,
as well as by your love, faith, and purity.

1 Timothy 4:12 CEV

We are halfway to Christmas.... May we be saved from being overly absorbed in the materialism and commercialization of the season, so that our hearts will be filled with the spirit and hope of Christ. O Lord God, keep us watchful for ways that we might ready the world and ourselves for Your rule. May we be strengthened and directed by the assurance of Your love and Your Holy Spirit, in Jesus' Name. Amen.

—James L. Christensen, *New Ways to Worship*

It is not enough to tell a child how to behave,
or how to find happiness. Words are plentiful.
Little lives are fragile. We must show them
in every gesture how to build a meaningful life,
how to extend our kindness to others and forgive cruelty
by doing so. We must show them how something
as easy as a smile can hold the power to heal.

—Corrine De Winter

December 15

Let us walk in the light of the Lord.

Isaiah 2:5

Father, we want our children to walk in your light. There are those who don't know you who would lead our offspring down paths we don't approve of. They lack the morals we are trying to instill in our children.

How can we shield our naive children from unsuitable companions? You know our children, Lord. Protect these precious young ones. Enter their hearts, and give them the strength to resist those who would mislead them.

Keep your children's eyes focused on God and their feet on his path.

December 16

Do not conform any longer to the pattern of this world,
but be transformed by the renewing of your mind. Then you will be able to
test and approve what God's will is—his good, pleasing and perfect will.

Romans 12:2 NIV

When tempted to stubbornly think "I can do this myself" and "I don't need to pray or ask God about this," it's wise to remember that God has promised to guide, not "over-rule" us.

Lord make thy will our will in all things.

—Dean Vaughan

December 17

In my distress and anguish, your commandments comfort me.

Psalm 119:143 TLB

The daily stresses—and sometimes the extra ones like sick kids, shedding dogs, broken washers and dryers, you name it—call for an immediate quiet moment with God.

December 18

Standing today, O God, upon sturdy ancestral roots that knew you as the Source of Life, I feel the need to thank all who came before me and to drop to my knees in gratitude to you.

Creating a family is like a building coming to life on graph paper, line by line, wall by wall, space by space. In the construction, make sure there are doors that swing both ways.

December 19

The godly people in the land are my true heroes! I take pleasure in them!

Psalm 16:3 NLT

Help me be creative but not condescending, O God, as I provide heroes for the children, looking past comic book characters and shallow media royalty to those who make a difference in their lives. It can be an exciting scavenger hunt, for there is much good.

How do you respect a child? Receive him, do not reject him. Try to like him, too. Let him have privacy. Let him think out loud without fear of being laughed at. Ask his opinions, desires, even advice.

—Wilda Fancher, *The Christian Woman in the Christian Home*

December 20

God be in my head, and in my understanding;
 God be in my eyes, and in my looking;
God be in my mount, and in my speaking;
God be in my heart, and in my thinking;
God be at my end, and at my departing.

—Old Sarum Primer

When teetering here on the "cutting edge" of technology, cyberspace, and everything in between, O God, it is reassuring to know that from the beginning of time, you guide, direct, and hear our voices as we continue to ask for guidance.

December 21

Even fools who keep silent are considered wise;
when they close their lips, they are deemed intelligent.

Proverbs 17:28

God, when I'm tempted to
answer questions the children
haven't even asked or give simple
answers when they need to discover something on their own,
gently shush my mouth and still
my thoughts. I am here to guide,
not to do everything.

It is a great thing to know the season
for speech and the season for silence.

—Seneca

December 22

As long as the earth endures, seedtime and harvest, cold and heat, summer and winter, day and night, shall not cease.

Genesis 8:22

e can relax, O Lord of light, on this the longest darkness of the year, knowing that in order for trees to blossom and bear fruit and the maple tree to yield its sugar, a resting stillness of dormancy is a welcome part of growth.

There is more in the darkness than things that go bump. It was a dark night when the "wise ones" followed a guiding star to the eternal light that no darkness has overcome.

December 23

The joy of God be in thy face,
Joy to all who see thee,
The circle of God around thy neck,
Angels of God shielding thee,
Angels of God shielding thee.

Joy of night and day be thine,
Joy of sun and moon be thine,
Joy of men and women be thine,
Each land and sea thou goest,
Each land and sea thou goest.

Be every season happy for thee,
Be every season bright for thee,
Be everyone glad for thee.
Thou beloved one of my breast.
Thou beloved one of my heart.

—Celtic Prayer

December 24

God so loved the world that he gave his only Son.

John 3:16

ompassionate and holy God, we celebrate your coming into this world. We celebrate with hope, we celebrate with peace, we celebrate with joy. Through your giving our lives are secure. Through your love we, too, can give love. You are the source of our being. Joy to the world!

The only gift is a portion of thyself.
—Ralph Waldo Emerson

December 25

*Do not be afraid; for see—I am bringing you good news
of great joy for all the people.*

Luke 2:10

God, on this most blessed day, I cannot contain the love in my heart for all you have given me: my spouse, my child, my family, and my friends. My heart is bursting with joy. Today I will celebrate the birth of your son and the birth of newfound happiness in my soul. Today I will honor the love you gave to the world and the love I, in turn, give to my own. Today I will rejoice in the gifts you have bestowed upon the earth and the gifts you have given to me. Thank you, God, for your love, for your light, for your son, for this day of glorious good tidings. Amen.

*In the eyes of those we love we see the
reflection of God looking back at us, smiling.
This is what it means to feel and to know joy.*

December 26

He said to them, "Why are you afraid? Have you still no faith?" And they were filled with great awe and said to one another, "Who then is this, that even the wind and sea obey him?"

Mark 4:40–41

Dear God,

This is the time of greatest darkness and the time of greatest light, when you gave your son to the world to shine forth as a beacon of love. Let me honor your gift at this holy time of year by promising to shine my own beacon of love upon my husband, my children, and my friends and neighbors. Let my joy spread to all those I meet along the way, and let my kindness touch every soul I come in contact with, just as your son did all those years ago. May I be to my children the guiding light that Jesus was to his disciples. Thank you, God, for sharing your beloved son with the world. Amen.

Mothers have the opportunity be the guiding light for their children. A child may look to many others for answers, for suggestions, for ideas, but only to his or her mother will a child look for the highest example of how to live.

December 27

If God is for us, who is against us? He who did not withhold his own Son, but gave him up for all of us, will he not with him also give us everything else?

Romans 8:31–32

Jesus, small poor baby of Bethlehem,
be born again in our hearts today;
be born again in our homes today;
be born again in our congregations today;
be born again in our neighborhoods today;
be born again in our cities today;
be born again in our nations today;
be born again in our world today.

Children need our presence more than they need our presents.... Blessed are those parents who learn the finer gift early on.

—Philip Gulley, *Front Porch Tales*

December 28

Loving Father, help us remember the birth of Jesus, that we may share in the song of the angels, the gladness of the shepherds and the wisdom of the wise men. Close the door of hate and open the door of love all over the world. Let kindness come with every gift and good desires with every greeting. Deliver us from evil by the blessing which Christ brings and teach us to be merry with clean hearts.

—Robert Louis Stevenson

The Child of glory
The Child of Mary
Born in the stable
The King of all,
Who came to the wilderness
And in our stead suffered;
Happy they are counted
Who to him are near.

—Celtic Prayer

December 29

Tomorrow is a day of solemn rest, a holy sabbath to the Lord.

Exodus 16:23

ear God, give us the courage to "unplug" on Sundays to replenish and enjoy the simple pleasures of one another's company. Keep us focused on your promised rest instead of on the world's distractions, at least for awhile.

Sweet hour of prayer, sweet hour of prayer,
That calls me from a world of care
And bids me at my Father's throne
Make all my wants and wishes known!
In seasons of distress and grief,
My soul has often found relief,
And oft escaped the tempter's snare
By thy return, sweet hour of prayer.

—William Walford, "Sweet Hour of Prayer"

December 30

Can any one of you by worrying add a single hour to your life?

Matthew 6:27 NIV

Like the littered house in the aftermath of the holidays, my soul is overcrowded. What, I worry, do I need to be a good mother?

Guide my sorting: Keep humor; toss battles of will. Keep tolerance and imagination; toss inflexibility and overreactive fear. Keep respect and acceptance of kids just as they are today; toss supermom lists and myths and others' expectations.

Guided by you, O God, my sorting will continue as I toss out useless worrying habits.

For God's children, useless worries are "leisure suits." Once fashionable, now outdated.

December 31

I am making all things new....
Write this, for these words are trustworthy and true.

Revelation 21:5

The past, O God of yesterdays, todays, and promise-filled tomorrows, can be an anchor or a launching pad. It's sometimes so easy to look back on the pain and hurt and believe the future may be an instant replay. Help us to accept the aches of the past and put them in perspective so we can also see the many ways you supported and nurtured us. Then, believing in your promise of regeneration, launch us into the future free and excited to live in joy.

The calendar is as bare as the Christmas tree, the page of tomorrow clean and ready. May God bless the New Year that beckons, helping us face what we must, celebrate every triumph we can, and make the changes we need. And now celebrate to the fullest this whistle-blowing, toast-raising moment, for it is the threshold between the old and new us.

My Prayer Life

ACKNOWLEDGMENTS

January 8, July 2, August 25, September 22, October 18, December 7: Excerpts from *Guide My Feet* by Marian Wright Edelman. Copyright © 1995 by Marian Wright Edelman. Reprinted by permission of Beacon Press, Boston.

January 12, February 8, April 29, May 30, June 27, July 6, August 28, September 2, November 13, December 14: Excerpts from *New Ways to Worship* by James L. Christensen. Used by permission of Fleming H. Revell, a division of Baker Book House Company, Copyright © 1973.

January 19: Excerpt from *Keep Me Faithful* by Ruth Harms Calkin, Pomona, California 91768. Used by permission. All rights reserved.

February 6, March 1: Excerpts from *Finding Hope Again* by Neil T. Anderson and Hal Baumchen. Copyright © 1999. Gospel Light/Regal Books, Ventura, California 93003. Used by permission.

February 16, May 12, May 23, June 12, August 8: Excerpts from *Waiting for a Miracle* by Jan Markell. Used by permission.

February 18: Excerpt from *A Mother's Joy* by June Masters Bacher. Used by permission.

February 23, June 5: Excerpts from *The Pursuit of God* by A.W. Tozer. Christian Publications, Camp Hill, Pennsylvania. Copyright © 1982, 1993. Used by permission.

March 7: Excerpt from *Life Is What You Make It* by Alfred Grant Walton. Baker Book House Company, Copyright © 1942.

March 10, June 11: Excerpts from *Things Pondered* by Beth Moore. Copyright © 1997 Beth Moore. All rights reserved. Used by permission.

March 11: "First Fig" from *Collected Poems* by Edna St. Vincent Millay, HarperCollins. Copyright © 1922, 1950 by Edna St. Vincent Millay.

March 15, May 7, June 16: Excerpts taken from *Boomerang Joy* by Barbara E. Johnson. Copyright © 1998 by Barbara E. Johnson. Used by permission of Zondervan Publishing House.

March 16, July 16, November 11: Excerpts from *Bless This Mess* by Jo Carr and Imogene Sorley. Copyright © 1969, Abingdon Press. Used by permission.

March 27, April 20, June 17: Excerpts from *Light for My Path*. Published by Barbour Publishing, Inc., Uhrichsville, Ohio. Used by permission.

April 14, July 20: Excerpts taken from *Heart Thoughts: A Treasury of Inner Wisdom* by Louise L. Hay. Copyright © 1990; Hay House, Inc., Carlsbad, California.

April 16, July 11: Taken from *Seasons of Your Heart* by Macrina Wiederkehr. Copyright © 1991 by Macrina Wiederkehr. Reprinted by permission of HarperCollins Publishers, Inc.